INTRODUCTION

"I Was Blessed, and Could Bless"

My fiftieth year had come and gone
I sat, a solitary man
In a crowded London shop
An open book and empty cup
On the marble table-top

While on the shop and street I gazed
My body of a sudden blazed
And twenty minutes more or less
It seemed, so great my happiness
That I was blessed, and could bless ...

—William Butler Yeats
"Vacillation"

When I was ten years old, my father began making a certain new gesture. It was after his father had died. I know for sure that my father had not made this gesture prior to my grandfather's death. It was a silent, almost unnoticeable gesture. For a split-second his eyes would glance upward—to the right and up—and sometimes he would smile. It was an intimate gesture that, it seemed, he thought no one else could see.

I knew in my heart that my father was glancing at his father, asking him to take notice of what was happening. My father made

1

this gesture rather often. He made it when something insignificantly wondrous happened: when my baby sister said or did something cute; when some incident was humorous or touching; when taut nerves were suddenly relaxed. Whenever these things happened—at the supper table, in the car, outdoors—my father's response was immediate and spontaneous. His glance was brief, exclusive to him and my grandfather, and I noticed it.

I felt the warmth and tenderness of my father's gesture. I knew he loved my grandfather. When my grandfather died, I saw my father cry for the first time. I knew he felt my grandfather's absence. My father's gesture, though, made my grandfather still present to me. Whenever I saw my father glance upward, I felt good. The gesture brought something into my life that hadn't been there before. The feeling lasted twenty minutes, more or less. Yet my father's gesture, made often, created a succession of these twenty minutes, and I knew that death was not just loss.

Death Brought into Daily Life

My grandfather's death caused my father to pay more attention to our daily life. The connection between my grandfather's death and my father's gesture brought death into the daily life we lived. Because of the warmth I felt between the two of them and because of the way I saw my father paying attention to the small happenings in our life, death became connected to a way of seeing for me. There was more communication after my grandfather died.

My father stopped making this gesture a few years after my grandfather died. Many years later I asked him about it. He told me that he had never realized he looked up and to the right. It wasn't that he had forgotten the gesture; it was simply that he had never been aware of it.

I had been, though. And now I make a similar gesture. I look at my father's photograph. It is the photograph we placed on his coffin when he died. When his photograph isn't around, I remember him, touch his St. Joseph medal that I wear around my neck, and acknowledge how he would appreciate this or that moment, this or that person. And I am blessed for twenty minutes, more or less. And I can bless.

The Misfit

Haunting the Human — Unveiling the Divine

God's Blessing,

Darlene

— F. Hary

The Misfit

Haunting the Human — Unveiling the Divine

LARRY LEWIS

ORBIS BOOKS
Maryknoll, New York 10545

Second Printing, July 1997

The Catholic Foreign Mission Society of America (Maryknoll) recruits and trains people for overseas missionary service. Through Orbis Books, Maryknoll aims to foster the international dialogue that is essential to mission. The books published, however, reflect the opinions of their authors and are not meant to represent the official position of the society.

Library of Congress Cataloging in Publication Data

Lewis, Larry, 1947–
    The misfit : haunting the human—unveiling the divine / Larry Lewis.
       p.   cm.
    Includes bibliographical references.
    ISBN 1-57075-122-6 (alk. paper)
    1. Lewis, Larry, 1947– . 2. Catholic Foreign Mission Society of America—Bibliography. 3. Missionaries—China—Wu-han shih—Biography. 4. Wu-han shih (China)—Description and travel. I. Title.
BX4705.L6172A3 1997
266′.2′092—dc21
  [B]   96-51865
                                       CIP

To
my father, Joe,
George Putnam, M.M.,
and Ina

Today the peonies in front of my steps,
Some are beginning to fade,
Some are beginning
to bloom.

When they bloom,
I do not understand why they are so
beautiful.
For when they fade,
we realize that they are like phantom
bodies.

How far is it from here
To the gateway to the void?

With these faded flowers,
let me come and ask you.

Po Chu-i (772–846)

CONTENTS

Permission from authors and publishers to reprint materials in *The Misfit* is gratefully acknowledged:

- to John Barth, M.M. for his sketch of the Gingko tree at Maryknoll Society Center, Maryknoll, N.Y.;

- to Kenneth Koch for Mary Tkalec's poem, which was orginally published in *I Never Told Anybody: Teaching Poetry Writing in a Nursing Home*, © 1977 by Kenneth Koch, published by Random House, 1977, p. 67;

- for selections from John Gardner, "Redemption," taken from *The Art of Loving and Other Stories*, New York: Alfred A. Knopf Publishers, 1981, pp. 30-48;

- for selections from *The Poems of W. B. Yeats: A New Edition*, reprinted with the permission of Simon and Schuster, edited by Richard J. Finneran, © 1933 by Macmillan Publishing Company, renewed 1961 by Bertha Yeats;

- for Ouyang Xiu's "The Huamei's Song" in *A Golden Treasury of Chinese Poetry*, translated by John A. Turner, S.J., published by Renditions Paperback, Hong Kong, 1989, p. 90;

- to Bette Midler for her monologue, "Fried Eggs" in *Bette Midler Live at Last*;

- to Marvin Bell for "These Green-Going-to-Yellow," which was first published in *The New Yorker* (3 November 1980, p. 56) and reprinted in *A Marvin Bell Reader*, Middlebury College Press/University Press of New England, © 1994 by Marvin Bell;

- to Harvard University Press for Emily Dickinson's "Blossoms will run away," reprinted by permission of the Publisher and the Trustees of Amherst College from *The Poems of Emily Dickinson*, edited by Thomas H. Johnson, Cambridge, Mass.: The Belknap Press of Harvard University Press, © 1951, 1955, 1979, 1983 by the President and Fellows of Harvard College.

Acknowledgements

Artists, authors and poets have long encouraged us through the misfits they have created. It is easy to imagine how people in their lives inspired them to transcend false and safe definitions. I thank those who fed the souls of Flannery O'Connor, Arthur Miller, and Alberto Giacometti who gave us "A Good Man is Hard to Find," *The Misfits,* and *Hands Holding the Void.*

To my mother Mary for seeing both sides of things; to my sister Joyce for her prevailing spirit; and to my sister Jude for housing me to write this book and for keeping my hunger alive and the demons creative—thank you.

For the constancy of their spirit I thank my fellow Maryknollers Tom Wilcox, John Kaserow, Frank Meccia, Xavier O'Donnell, Elizabeth Conroy, and Ray Pierini.

To Grace Meyerjack and Chuck Maes for the walk toward the void; to Scott Harris for the confidence; to Giuseppe Vignato for the gaze toward God; and to Anthony Ferro for the honesty—my gratitude.

I pray the students and teachers of Wuhan University of Technology, 1988–1991, know how they brought me back to God.

Finally my thanks to Bill Burrows of Orbis Books for his encouragement, perseverance and appreciation (from our first conversation) of what I've tried to convey, to Celine Allen for her *art* of editing, and to Catherine Costello for her caring production work.

Names of Chinese colleagues and friends mentioned in this book have been changed.

The moments of sudden blazing when happiness is so great that we feel blessed and can, in turn, bless are often associated with some form of emptiness. The fiftieth year, the solitary man in a crowded shop, the open book or empty cup allow a clear-sightedness that emptiness alone can create.

My daily life as a child was blessed through my father's glance toward his deceased father. My father's loss was my daily blessing. His loss sparked his sight; he paid more attention. He was seeing for two people. I am sure that insignificantly wondrous things happened before my grandfather died. My sister was cute and did precious things. Taut nerves were relaxed. Yet, before my grandfather died, my father had no need to glance upward.

I know how a father's death can affect a son. When my father died, every moment of past vulnerability flooded in on me. Childhood fears and insecurities returned. Old scars I thought had healed opened up again. It was worse than feeling like a child, because I was an adult. I found myself looking to my father's photograph, not only for strength and understanding, but also to ask him to see what was happening in my life now: new things, new people, new ventures. I found myself taking the initiative to ask him to see and to bless.

My ability to bless now, however, is always tinged by the emptiness I have felt since his death. He isn't here; I cannot talk with him. I no longer hear the timbre of his voice. Sometimes I forget him and then suddenly notice the shape of the head of the man driving the car ahead of me. He looks like my father. And then I remember again that my father is dead. I remember what happened yesterday or last week and how I would have told him things if he had been here. And I make the effort to remember his voice and his smell and his way of seeing life.

The Disrupting Stretch toward the Void
Brings Clarity of Vision

The hole left by my father's absence takes away some of the stuff of life that can obscure truer vision. I see better now. I take notice and want him to also. His smell, his shoulder, and his strength are gone, and at times I find myself stretching for them to feel more secure or to feel the company of an understanding, loving man. Sometimes when I stretch I discover that, while I miss him, I can give myself what he had provided in the past. His absence forces me to stand more on my own feet. I don't know which is more startling: to stretch and not find him here or to stretch and find that I can provide for myself. In any case, the stretching is always there; it comes through his death. Sometimes the stretch is acknowledged, sometimes it isn't, but it is always present.

There is no doubt in my mind that the stretch is within all of us. We want things to come together, to fit, to make sense, to remain the same. We want things in their proper place. We want to know where and how we belong. We want no disruption in the order we've grown familiar with and on which we rely. The dislocation and disruption that come through the death of a loved one jar us out of how we thought we fit and move us into the truth of the void in each of our lives. Try as we might, nothing can fill this void.

Something always calls forth and addresses the void. Often it is emptiness that evokes the void and with it the question of life's meaning. The stretch each of us makes, whether toward or away from the void, addresses the truth that we do not belong to this life alone. The glance upward and to the right that seeks blessing from beyond, the look toward the photograph that feels the absence and longs for presence, or the pause of wonder that comes unsolicited and elicits amazement all remind us that there is more to this life than that to which we are accustomed. The stretch reminds us that we do not belong to this life alone.

Misfitness: Gateway into the Void

Death is perhaps the most blatant reminder that we do not fit into this life. There is, however, a more subtle reminder of the void that indicates we do not belong to this life alone. It is a social "misfitness" that, if we are honest, each of us felt early on in life. This social misfitness is nearly as undeniable as death. It is also nearly as uncomfortable as death. Its effects and presence in daily life, though, are more available to us than is death. Because this misfitness, unique to each person, is a social phenomenon, we felt (and still feel) its ostracizing power. The hole it created has left its mark on our souls.

Social misfitness is usually associated with having too much or too little of something. We were too fat or too thin, too ugly or too good looking, too tall or too short, too neglected or loved too much, too poor or too rich. We felt removed from others and that distance created the hole, the interior void, on a social level. Along with the awareness of the distance between ourselves and others came the need to stretch for the sake of trying to fit in, to belong or to deny that we didn't belong.

In addition to the social misfitness we felt as children, the wonder we experienced has also left its mark on our souls. Wonder too can bring us to the brink of feeling a sacredness within that has been dormant and waiting to be acknowledged. Who hasn't felt the wonder of seeing the stars for the first time in a sky that was always above us? The noise of the wind, the sound of a creek in the back yard, the beauty of budding flowers, a friendship enjoyed—all create spaces in our souls and open us to more than we had thought possible. These spaces are never filled, and their emptiness calls us to be more fully alive. We stretch toward these spaces all too infrequently to let their richness and silence remind us of what could be.

Both forms of misfitness—being too much this or too little that and feeling the wonder that takes us beyond what we have known—are gateways to the void. Both forms of misfitness emerged when we were children and didn't have the knowledge, skills, or understanding to keep them at bay. Stretching toward these spaces can be painful or exhilarating or sometimes both. Regardless of the pain or the exhilaration, the created spaces belong to us; they are ours. How we regard them and what we do with these voids will either cut us off from or draw us toward that which they bespeak.

The book of our lives is supposed to be readable, within our control and not too revelatory to ourselves or to others. We are supposed to feel full and satisfied. We are supposed to fit into the crowd, to belong and not be seen as solitary. Yet, when we've lived long enough to know that the book is open and the cup is undeniably empty and the crowd no longer suffices to attract us, the void created by our social misfitness awaits. It has always been there; we have turned away.

Does the waiting void offer any direction to the aimlessness we finally let ourselves feel? Are we, like Yeats, prepared to see in a manner that sets us ablaze? Does the emptiness of the void created by our social misfitness prepare us to see, to be blessed and to bless?

My father's glance toward his father connected me to the gateway of the void. I felt blessed through my father's loss because of what I saw him do with it. How can we grow more confident that stretching toward the void will make us more alive? Can something so seemingly negative as not fitting in socially and something so quantitatively worthless as glancing upward be mirrors to us of what it means to be more fully alive?

The void created through social misfitness haunts us. The haunting draws us to the gateway of the void. What lies beyond and who or what can guide us to stretch toward rather than away from the void that beckons?

1

"WHERE WINDS MEET"

The Gateway of the Misfit

I asked her if the recent rains were causing pain in her leg that had been broken two summers ago. She smiled and said, "Oh, no. The doctor gave me some new medicine. Let me show you." She reached far down into her baggy pants pocket and rummaged around. A little embarrassed at the time it was taking to find the medicine, she started to laugh, her eyes twinkling. Then she pulled out her hand and held up a dead bird.

I was speechless, and she seemed as surprised as I was. She peered at the bird and said, "Where did that come from?" Then she matter-of-factly put it on the coffee table and reached again into her pocket. She found the medicine, showed me, and put the medicine back into her pocket. We continued talking and drinking tea. The dead bird remained on the table next to the gift of cookies and spring rolls she had brought. She never came empty-handed to visit.

The place was my apartment on the campus of Wuhan University of Technology in China where I taught for three years, 1988–91. The woman was Xie Lau Shi (Teacher Xie). I called her Xie Lau Shi; no one else did. She was responsible for discipline on the campus. She proudly wore a red armband with yellow lettering on it. It gave her an identity. The job had obviously been created for her. People spoke of her behind her back and thought she was crazy. The first time we met, I thought she was crazy too.

A Gardenia, a Sacrament

When we first met, I had been teaching in China for only two weeks. It was a hot September morning. I had a twenty-minute break between mid-morning classes, so I joined some students who were sitting on a grassy area between classroom buildings.

All of a sudden I heard someone raging and screaming in the distance behind me. The uncontrolled, insane-sounding voice was getting closer and closer. I could make out some of what she was yelling in Chinese, "Who do you think you are? Not listening to me! Not obeying the rules!"

I knew everyone was looking in her direction. All the students in the area were silent. I wanted to turn around so I could find out who this maniac was and see the poor soul who was the object of her wrath. My Western etiquette, however, kept me from doing this. She was getting closer. Suddenly, I felt a forceful poke in the middle of my back!

I turned around, not understanding why I should be the object of this woman's rage. My shock was equalled by hers. Viewed from behind, I could pass for a Chinese. As I turned, though, her wrath was met by my long nose! She exclaimed, "Eh? *Lau Wai!*" (What? A foreigner!) Her face changed expression in an instant. The red of rage turned to the red of embarrassment. The scowl turned into the twinkle-eyed smile I would come to love during my time in Wuhan.

She didn't attempt to explain why she had been ranting so. (I later learned we weren't supposed to sit on the grassy area.) She didn't even stop to consider whether or not I could speak Chinese. She merely asked me where I came from and offered me an official welcome to the university. I expressed my gratitude for the welcome. I knew she was not quite "normal."

Everyone there that morning laughed at her and was embarrassed for her having embarrassed me. Using the polite form of Chinese, I asked her family name. She responded with a smile, using the humble form in telling me that her family name was Xie. I said, "I am happy to meet you Teacher Xie." (I addressed anyone on campus who was obviously not a student as "Teacher" to save them and myself a loss of face.) Everyone laughed again at my response because, as I would discover, no one ever referred to her as "Teacher Xie."

The footpath news of our meeting that morning spread quickly throughout the small world of the university. Later that month, one of the university's vice presidents passed by as I was walking to class. He mentioned Xie, using her given name along with her family name. At first I didn't recognize who he was referring to. Then I said, "Oh, you mean Xie Lau Shi." He nodded in agreement. I noticed a hint of puzzlement on his face, but he didn't want to correct me. He then apologized gracefully for her having singled me out and shouting at me. I assured him there was no problem.

Initially it struck me as odd that, of all the people I came to know and love in China, Xie Lau Shi is the one most in my thoughts now. Looking back on the three years, however, it seems fitting that a misfit such as she would hold prominence in my memory. To a significant degree she represents and brings forth both my love for the Chinese people and what inspires my vocation as a foreign missioner.

The day I left Wuhan reveals on a deeper level how this woman touched me as a human being and, therefore, as a foreign missioner. As I mentioned, Xie Lau Shi was in charge of university discipline. I would often hear her screaming as I walked to and from classes. Sometimes I would pass by her and see the unfortunate victim forced to listen to her. If faculty children or university students had committed some act that she considered disrespectful toward the campus (picking flowers, littering, or engaging in play she deemed inappropriate), and if she was in one of her moods, Xie Lau Shi would start her harangue. Circles of people would often surround her and her victim.

About one week before I was due to leave, I was going to the dining hall for supper. The campus had many huge and beautiful gardenia bushes. Those near the dining hall were unusually full; they were considered prize bushes for stealing gardenias for girl friends and mothers. That day, Xie Lau Shi was standing by the bushes scolding two primary school children whom she had caught with several gardenias in their hands. She saw me coming, quickly ended her tirade on respect for the campus, and took the flowers from the children. "Lau Wung, *gei nin*," she said as she smiled and gave me the flowers. (Wung is my Chinese family name. What she said, using the polite form, was, "Old Wung, for you.") I felt a little ashamed carrying the flowers into the dining room.

One week later I was preparing to leave. I had spent three years at the university, one year before and two years after the June 4, 1989, Tiananmen massacre. The people at the university felt comfortable with me and I with them. They knew that I loved them, and I was grateful for that. We had lived through many things, both ordinary and extraordinary, together. We had a history.

On the morning I was to leave, the students I had taught gathered outside my apartment. They had come to say good-bye. Some university officials, the chairs of the Foreign Languages Department, and the university's Foreign Affairs Office directors were also outside the apartment. I cried, as did they.

As I climbed into the van to go to the airport, I heard people saying, "Xie Lau Shi... Xie Lau Shi is coming..." I looked out the van window and saw the crowd of people separating to let Xie Lau Shi get to the van. All I could think of was Moses parting the Red Sea. Xie Lau Shi ran up to the window and reached in with a gardenia she had picked. Her twinkling eyes were tear-filled. "For you," she said. I took the gardenia and pressed it into my passport folder.

Now the flower is beautifully framed together with two white paper flowers that were hung on trees in the campus square during a memorial service conducted by the students two years earlier for those killed at Tiananmen. Xie Lau Shi's gardenia and the white paper flowers are my sacraments from my three years in China.

Xie Lau Shi is a misfit in Chinese culture and society. She does not fit within the norms set by her country's culture, tradition, and history, or by the Communist Party. I remember one day when, in an intensified moment of clarity familiar to anyone who knows a person said to be "crazy," she looked me straight in the eyes and said, "I was different before the Cultural Revolution." My heart was pierced that day for her. She never mentioned anything like that again.

Many of the students and faculty spoke often to me about current and past Chinese history and how the abuse of power oppressively affects all aspects of their thought and especially their behavior. Although Xie Lau Shi was an obvious misfit because of her inability to establish and maintain a facade acceptable in Chinese culture and society, 99 percent of the university population were also misfits. The university students were more subtle misfits because they could think for themselves and question the society into which they would soon try to fit. They could engage in appropriate behavior that allowed them to play the game of society.

In China I was an eyesore. Nothing about me fit. My nose betrayed any attempt I might make—through language study, study of Chinese philosophy, or adaptation to Chinese society and etiquette—to fit in. Such attempts are absolutely necessary, and any respectful missioner will spend a lifetime in their pursuit. Yet, ever and always, the foreign missioner remains a misfit in the host culture.

In my home culture I am a less obvious misfit. My values, my ways of perceiving, and, I hope, my way of living mark me as one who does not completely buy into the American dream. Nevertheless, in my home culture I am familiar with ways that allow me to hide my misfitness. No one need know that I do not necessarily believe in the American dream.

When, in my home culture, I remember my social misfitness, I can find support in certain aspects of my life that might be considered subcultural in the United States. For example, I can focus on my spiritual life or seek out people who have similar values. My social misfitness can become a compass or guide that draws me toward my truer self.

However, when I want to forget that I do not fit, when remembering my social misfitness is unbearable, my home culture provides escapes galore toward which I can run. Films are in English and have no subtitles; newspapers, magazines, and television are always at hand. It is easy for me to forget my own social misfitness and the fact that the void is at the heart of being human.

The Waiting Void

In China, however, reminders of my social misfitness surround me. The void that follows this awareness is more present to me.

Attempts at fitting, which are, after all, an expression of the missionary vocation, can also be a betrayal of it. This is because my attempts to fit in can be motivated by trying to forget, to deceive myself that I do belong—not only in China but to this life alone.

In China, when the void is too present to me, my attempts at escape require more energy than they do in my home culture. Films are subtitled. Street scenes and smells, television, newspapers, and magazines all carry the message that I am not Chinese. My home is not here. Where is it?

Foreign missioners carry this question with them more intensely and more consistently than do most people. At moments of death, or when extreme life change or crisis or art punctures through the shell of looking good, most people face the question of their true home. The vocation of foreign mission carries with it the void that waits behind felt social misfitness, the void that announces, "Home is elsewhere!"

The Xie Lau Shis of every culture also bring with them the reminder of the void. Obvious social misfits carry with them the truth that they cannot be defined or contained by the socio-cultural norms of their home cultures. We've all met Xie Lau Shis in our home cultures.

I recall walking the streets of Pittsburgh alone on a hot July afternoon. It was so hot that no one else was out. What made this particular day so memorable for me was the fact that I had just realized what it meant to have 340 pages of my doctoral dissertation labeled "total rewrite necessary." My draft had been returned to me in April with that message. I had laughed it off at first and then tried for two months to patch it up. Finally, in July, I accepted the overwhelming truth that a total rewrite was indeed necessary. I felt like a freak walking the streets of Pittsburgh that hot, sunny afternoon. I didn't look like the outcast I felt like inside.

Then I noticed a woman dressed in a black overcoat, a black kerchief, black pants, and black gloves. She was yelling something about God. Although she was walking toward me, she was on the opposite side of the street. Suddenly, I saw her start to cross the street toward me. I thought of running from her, but decided against it. It would be just my luck that day that she'd come after me. She came up to me, still shouting, "Do you know God?" Her face—which was inches from mine—was all wrinkled; I was amazed that such an elderly person could scream so loudly.

"Yes," I answered quietly, hoping she'd take the cue from me that she didn't need to shout.

"Do you know why He sent His Son?" she asked just as loudly.

"Yes," I said, hoping she'd be satisfied and walk past me now.

"Why?" She wasn't letting up with the questions or the volume.

"Because He loves us."

Then she looked through my eyes into my soul and almost whispered in her Eastern European accent, "You good boy."

I ran home, leaned up against the cool wall and asked myself, "Who's crazy?" This encounter happened fourteen years ago in my home culture. An obvious social misfit had stopped me in my self-pity and near despair at having to face a total rewrite. Her black, heavy clothing, her loud proclamation about God on a hot, deserted sidewalk in Pittsburgh had carried me back to myself. Her void was showing for all the world to see. Mine was kept hidden, albeit with tremendous effort.

Social misfits carry their stories with them. I never knew this woman's story. Nor did I completely know that of Xie Lau Shi. I knew mine somewhat, or at least I knew the social implications of having to rewrite 340 pages. I had not lived up to my own expectations and I had let down those who were supporting me. This screaming missioner dressed in black had illuminated some of my social misfitness so that I could see beneath it to the void where I knew something was waiting for me. I remember her and am thankful for what she said. She evoked from me a deeper truth that didn't rewrite the dissertation but did keep me mindful, for twenty minutes, more or less, of something more important.

Foreign missioners are misfits regardless of the culture in which they live and work. Having lived, worked, and loved in both home and host cultures, they feel at home in neither. Missioners arriving in a host culture see that culture from an outsider's viewpoint. They also take into their lives values of the host culture that reveal less than satisfactory truths about their home culture.

When I first got to China, I couldn't tolerate how most of the people would stare openly at anyone who didn't fit the norm. Conformity is held in such high regard there that anyone who sticks out for any reason is gawked at. At least in the States we try to hide that aspect.

On the other hand, relationships in China mean more. People sit and talk with each other. Small graces mean more when time is put aside for sitting and talking with the person you pass on the street. When I returned to the States and saw this small grace absent, I felt that my home country was less than appreciative of something so important as the value of spending time with people.

These small graces, rhythms of time and social relations that missioners see in both home and host cultures give them a unique vantage point. The vantage point is that they see, live, and love the truth that they belong to neither culture. All missioners feel that the culture shock upon returning to their home culture is often more painful than that of going to the host culture for the first time.

Recent and future generations of foreign missioners are and will be exposed to living and loving more frequently between cultures. In the past, missioners often remained in the missions for most of their lives. Now, with fewer vocations, commitments in home cultures, and the availability and convenience of travel, missioners have both the need and the ability to live and move more frequently between cultures. Therefore, they will also be more exposed to their geographical/cultural misfitness. How will they respond to this increased awareness?

I was talking recently with a foreign missioner. He told me that as he lives between cultures, he feels as if he's caught in a place "where the winds meet." I thought this an apt description. The winds of two vastly different cultures meet in the individual lives of foreign missioners. The turbulence created by the winds in the lives of foreign missioners opens them, through their social misfitness, to the void, the eye of the storm. The silence of the void can remind them how their vocation is connected to the fundamental vocation of what it means to be human. As human beings, we live in this world. The gateway of the void opens us to the other world, eternity, toward which we all are tending.

The void brought into awareness through any form of social misfitness brings all people to the remembrance of the beyond.

When we are brought to this awareness, not only is our vision more illusion-free, but, as a result, our true human vocation has the opportunity to shine forth. I know from my own experience and that of others that we live more genuinely when something happens that stops our usual way of living as if we fit this world alone.

When, less than two months after my father had been diagnosed with cancer and one month before he died, my older sister was also diagnosed with cancer, everything in my life stopped. The threat of death and death itself put an end to the illusion that I fit in.

I remember very clearly on the many visits to my mother and sister during those months how the toll-taker on the New York State Thruway could affect my life. If he smiled a "thank you," I felt encouraged and touched by his kindness. If he was too busy or perhaps having a bad day and didn't take the time to nod or to smile, I felt unsupported in my time of vulnerability. I felt raw and was aware of feeling raw. The changes in our family highlighted every act and every person I encountered. I both hated and cherished those months.

Today I both hate and cherish my normal life of fitting in. I pass the toll booth on the Thruway now and remember those feelings. In a way, the toll booth is a sacrament, just as Xie Lau Shi's gardenia and the students' white paper flowers are.

Memories of the months of rawness when our family was threatened are evoked when I am faced with the Xie Lau Shis, the black-clothed screaming missioners on the street, the kind toll-takers, the Tiananmen atrocities, and the sound of the creek in the back yard. Misfits and acts that jar us out of the feeling that we fit into this life connect us to the ultimate truth that we were not created for this life alone. Wasting time and energy to maintain the illusion that we do fit in is maintaining a lie. As Anne Morrow Lindbergh says,

> In the end one has to discard shields and remain open and vulnerable. Otherwise, scar tissue will seal off the wound and no growth will follow. To grow, to be reborn, one must remain vulnerable—open to love but also hideously open to the possibility of more suffering.[1]

When my usual life of trying to fit in is threatened, I am reminded I was not created to be limited by the norms that dictate
what it is to fit in.

The Two Journeys and the Two Worlds of the Missioner

Foreign missioners straddle two cultures. Their straddling demands that they stretch geographically and interiorly:

> The geographical pilgrimage is the symbolic acting out
> of an inner journey. The inner journey is the interpolation
> of the meanings and signs of the outer pilgrimage. One
> can have one without the other. It is better to have both.
> History would show the fatality and doom that would at-
> tend on the external pilgrimage with no interior spiritual
> integration, a divisive and disintegrated wandering, with-
> out understanding and without the fulfillment of any
> humble inner quest. In such pilgrimage no blessing is
> found within, and so the outward journey is cursed with
> alienation.[2]

Stretching that spans two cultures and two journeys points to
the ultimate journey of life. Chinese philosophy addresses those
who can synthesize the winds of the fundamental stretch between
this world and the other:

> According to Chinese philosophy, the man who accom-
> plishes this synthesis, not only in theory but also in deed,
> is the sage. He is both this-worldly and other-worldly.
> The spiritual achievement of the Chinese sage corre-
> sponds to the saint's achievement in Buddhism, and in
> Western religion. But the Chinese sage is not one who
> does not concern himself with the business of the world.
> His character is described as one of "sageliness within
> and kingliness without." That is to say, in his inner sage-
> liness, he accomplishes spiritual cultivation; in his kingli-
> ness without, he functions in society.[3]

Foreign missioners' lives are the locale where the winds meet: the winds of two cultures and the winds of two worlds. Because of this, foreign missioners are profoundly connected to the fundamental mystery of humanity. While serving as beacons for the misfits of this world, they in turn receive direction from the very same misfits. In this is the mirroring. It is the mirroring of the saints:

> The artist, the thinker, the hero, the saint—who are they, finally, but the finite self radicalized and intensified? The difference between the artist and the rest of us is one of intense degree, not one of kind. The difference is one where the journey of intensification—a journey which most of us fear yet desire, shun yet demand—is really undertaken.[4]

The sage, the saint, the artist and, finally, the missioner are those who undertake the intensified journey. They expose themselves to the more consistent reminder, through stretching between cultures and worlds, that their misfittedness is their grace. Bishop James Edward Walsh of Maryknoll began his "Description of a Missioner" with:

> It is better to be a saint than a good missioner; but is it easier? This is a scandalizing question, but it has an edifying answer that magnifies the missioner without belittling the saint. And the missioner has need of a little magnifying, for a low view of his calling is his greatest danger. He tends to think of himself as one sent, rather than as one called...He is not a saint, but he is so seriously involved in the implications of sanctity that it behooves him to study his own lesser vocation in the light of the greater one.[5]

Called to be beacons for the misfits whose lives carry the void that brings them to the gateway of eternity, foreign missioners need some magnifying of their call. Indeed, it is in the mirror of the misfits that foreign missioners are reminded that they have been called and sent by Jesus, a misfit who stretched *toward* rather than *away from* the waiting void of God's promise. Jesus' life, death, and resurrection offer not protection but the sustenance, the radical support of knowing that God's promise is best remembered in the void.

In this work we shall see how the vocation of the foreign missioner intimately supports the human mystery to live life more fully by stretching toward the void wherein waits divine love.

2
"WHERE IS GREEN?"

The Question Asked Again

Where is Green?
Land, mountain, ocean—
I'm always thinking,
Looking for green.

In my childhood memories
Everything's green in Spring—
Green on the land,
Green in the mountain,
Green in the ocean.
The whole world is filled with green.

Grown up now,
I'm puzzled because
Not every corner is green.
War, disease, deception.

Where is green?
But for the peace of green
I'm waiting.[1]

I went to China in August of 1988, ten months after my father had died. My older sister had undergone two surgical procedures for cancer, and her radiation therapy was completed eight months before I left. We had moved my mother into a new apartment two months prior to my departure. I had been on sabbatical since the summer of 1987, trying to adapt my doctoral dissertation on "Waiting" into a book for publication.

Before the sabbatical I had been teaching in our graduate school of theology and serving as one of the spiritual directors for Maryknoll's seminarians. At the beginning I loved my assignment and found it personally enriching. Not only did I have a superb spiritual director and an excellent group of colleagues to work with, but the teaching dovetailed my personal and professional life at the time.

Then new appointments were made and new policies were developed that called into question much of what I valued professionally and personally. As sometimes happens, I found myself on the "political outs" with the new regime under which I was now expected to work.

I spent three years teaching under the new arrangement. The working situation and what I experienced as a struggle to maintain my integrity left me dry and indifferent. I felt incongruent and hypocritical: I was involved in teaching spirituality and the ministry of spiritual direction, but I felt surrounded by deceit, paralyzed by my anger, and disillusioned by my naivete. The sabbatical came at a good time for me and for those in charge at the time. I knew they were just as happy as I was that I was getting out of the picture.

In the spring of 1987 I was invited to give retreats to our missioners in Japan, Korea, Taiwan, and Hong Kong during the autumn months of 1988. The invitation had come before the sabbatical began and before our family was touched by death. I was looking forward to the retreats. I enjoyed being with my fellow Maryknollers on that level; it was as free of politics as any situation could be.

However, as the time approached in mid-summer of 1988 to begin preparing the retreats, I felt I was the least qualified person to offer them. I knew I was spiritually indifferent and dead. In less than a year's time I found life and myself drastically changed. My book had been stillborn; I had been too close to my father's death, my sister's cancer, and the Maryknoll situation to write anything worthwhile. I had spent most of the year in the car, traveling to visit my mother and my older sister. I felt guilty for having wasted

Maryknoll's time and money. I cried nearly every day over my father's death. Worry over my sister's cancer, anger at the unfairness of it, and concern for my mother's future had left me drained. The only good that came of that time was the mutually supportive relationship my younger sister and I developed. I knew I no longer thought of her as my younger sister; we had become pillars for each other.

On July 6, 1988, two months before the end of my sabbatical, something totally unexpected happened: I received a letter inviting me to teach English at Wuhan University of Technology in China! I had planned to go to China in the autumn of 1989; responding to this invitation would move my schedule up by a year.

In 1986 I had met a professor from Wuhan who was visiting Maryknoll. He had been the personal secretary of our Bishop James Edward Walsh in the early 1950s. When I took him to Bishop Walsh's grave to pay his respects, this man, who was in his late sixties, took off his hat; one tear fell from his eyes. That moment at Bishop Walsh's gravesite created an instant friendship between us. He asked if he could do anything for me. I told him I wanted to go to China to teach beginning in autumn of 1989. I gave him my resume, and he promised to help. I knew this professor did not teach at Wuhan University of Technology, but I assumed he had sent my resume to that school thinking I wanted to begin teaching in autumn 1988. His "mistake" in time was providential.

To say that I was thrilled to receive this invitation because I had entered Maryknoll to go to mainland China would be a lie. True, I did enter Maryknoll to go one day to mainland China. My four years in Taiwan had been a delight; I had thoroughly enjoyed the people and my work there. Yet always in my mind and heart was the hope that one day I could work in mainland China. The invitation that came so unexpectedly in the summer of 1988 could have been the fulfillment of that dream. But I was thrilled mainly because it offered me an out from the retreats, from all things spiritual, and from mourning and its aftermath.

After consulting with my superiors at Maryknoll and scrambling to find replacements for the retreats on such short notice, I was assigned to our Hong Kong Region and wrote to Wuhan University of Technology accepting the teaching position for the autumn of 1988. I waited and waited to hear from Wuhan, but nothing came in the mail. I telephoned incessantly, but could not get through. I began getting my shots, boosters, and HIV test, but without a letter of contract I could obtain only a tourist visa from the Chinese Embassy. I was to go to China not knowing if I definitely had a job in Wuhan.

I didn't care. In addition to the out offered by the July 6th invitation was the appeal of teaching at a university of technology. I was interested in and more than content with the prospect of teaching grammar, conversation, spelling—anything and everything that had no content or meaning of any sort. I needed, wanted, and felt qualified to teach anything that dealt with nothing. I had joined Maryknoll to proclaim the Gospel; I was finally going to China but I knew I was going to escape.

I vividly remember getting on the plane to Hong Kong. I felt as if I were stepping off a cliff into darkness. I had left home twice before on assignment to Taiwan. The pain of separation will always be with missioners at each departure. It gets worse, in fact, with aging loved ones. The pain this time was compounded by the horror of knowing full well why I was going: to leave everything and everyone behind.

Feelings of sadness, pain, guilt, and a sense of abandoning one's family do accompany missioners when we depart. To acknowledge these feelings with care and keep one's hand to the plow is the call. I acknowledged, and I cared. I gripped the plow, though, not in response to the call, but in direst need. It was the only thing that could take me away with "some face" in my Maryknoll family—the other family that I was escaping. Evangelization for the sake of escaping—hardly a pure motivation, but it was mine at the time. I wanted an out, and it was given to me on July 6, 1988.

On the plane, I re-read a letter my younger sister had written me on July 18th, shortly after I knew for certain that I had arranged on my end the go-ahead for China. The place where I re-read her letter, mid-air, was the most apt description of my state at the time. Of all the people I was leaving, she was the one I most needed to take with me:

> Try to understand my reserve. It's just that our hands have parted, the grip loosened. My palm still clammy, yours now drying. Our stance shifted—you see what I

cannot. I feel what you cannot. You're leaving. Another loss. Harden up—more change.

You say that the changes involved in going overseas are akin, somehow, to death. For whom? The one leaving or the ones left? Both?

Muscles worn from "adjustment," pulled from "carrying on"—frayed faith has me believing that "of course, I'll be okay."

Please try to understand. You've left already. I'm left already. I am happy for your happiness, but that is beneath this skin, hard from the protection of loss, that I must shed. It will be a while. You may be gone by that time. I'm so sorry I can't share it with you yet. Please try to understand. My heart hurts—I will miss you now, too.

Such extremities, why aren't I numb? Another absence at the festive table. Why do I anticipate the pain? Am I that selfish? I am right now... I'm so tired from my bristling exterior. It takes so much work to be this hard. I don't know how to be otherwise, yet... We were such a team for 365 days. It feels too soon to "lose" another... I'm scared to go solo; I already feel so profoundly alone. Your seat, still warm, next to me in our boat. I'll navigate on my own with your strengths always beside me. Will I be enough? As pain-filled as this year was, we all had the gift of each other's love as the backdrop to all tears, laughs, impatience, spats... So, I suppose, rather than a loss, I should view your leaving as a return to the norm?... I want so badly to share your happiness as much as I am able from my fundamentally different-from-yours stance.

I thought I was leaving all those feelings behind, but how could I? How could it have been possible?

"Hang on, kid. Be patient."

I arrived in Hong Kong in late August and telephoned Wuhan. The job was mine. Shortly before leaving the States I had learned that another Maryknoll priest, Father George Putnam, would also be teaching at Wuhan University of Technology that year. George was seventy-nine at the time. He had taught in China for a few years before the Communists had come into power. After that, he had taught sociology in the college seminary both in the United States for several years (I had him during my junior year) and in East Africa for nineteen years.

George went back to China as soon as it was possible to do so; China was his first love. His enthusiasm touched me, convincing me of my desire to go to China. The last time I had seen him had been in the summer of 1986 when I was passing through Hong Kong. George had just completed a six-month teaching contract at a university in northern China and was about to go to another university on a one-year contract. He ended up staying there for two years but was unable to return because of his advanced age. Somehow, though, he had now managed to secure a position in Wuhan.

I was happy that George and I would be together. I had always respected and liked him. He was a young-minded man, a fervent Democrat with a keen mind and a wonderful sense of humor. He enjoyed life, had a good eye for and loved people, and was a gentleman. Neither of us had planned on the other being at Wuhan University of Technology. It just worked out that way.

George and the assistant director of the university's Foreign Affairs Office met me at the airport on August 31, 1988. George had arrived earlier that day. It was stifling hot, humid, and rainy. George shook my hand and said, "Hang on, kid. Be patient." I asked him what he meant. He said I'd soon see.

Our accommodations were like a bomb shelter: moldy, rancid, dirty, dark, and dank. We each had an apartment in the same building, with separate outside entrances leading to the second floor where we were to live. Each apartment had two bedrooms, a living room, a Western-style toilet, tub and shower, and a small kitchen. It had sounded great in the letter, but seeing and smelling it was far different.

Across the hall from me there was another apartment where a Chinese family lived. The Chinese family and I used the same outside entrance. All the apartments in this building were on the second floor; the first floor apartments had been gutted and earth, broken glass, and mold filled the entire first-floor space.

George and I got more or less settled and then went out to a local restaurant for supper. It was pitch black when we returned and we had difficulty trying to find our way to the apartment building. All of a sudden right next to us we heard a young Chinese woman ask us in Chinese if we were the two new foreign teachers and if we were lost. I told her we were. She kindly led us to our building.

George got into his entrance all right, but mine was bolted shut from the inside. I knocked and banged and shouted in Chinese for the people upstairs sharing my entrance to open the door. A man in his thirties came down; he had obviously been sleeping. I apologized for having awakened him. He groggily said, "No matter." This was how I met the son of the matriarch who lived across the hall from me with her family.

When I got into my apartment, I just took off my clothes and collapsed on the moldy bed. No towels or toilet paper were provided. I fell asleep sweaty and dirty, thinking, "What am I doing here?" Then I quickly recalled that I had nowhere else to go.

At 6:10 the next morning I was awakened by the campus loudspeaker blaring the song from the film "Flashdance." It was almost comical. I washed my face and brushed my teeth. No coffee. The Foreign Affairs man had told us that we were to get physicals and have photographs taken that day so that we could obtain work visas. The work visa would enable us to get several other IDs we would need. We were also to meet with the Foreign Languages Department chairs and curriculum director to get our courses, texts and teaching schedules.

As I headed downstairs to go to George's apartment, I saw a large dish of wet garbage on the landing outside my Chinese neighbor's door. I tried not to think about the rats that I knew must be somewhere nearby. My first night and first morning in China had left me feeling cynical, and I knew I would be looking for reasons not to like the place.

We went to the provincial clinic for the physicals. It was a scene from a Three Stooges episode. The doctor, with dyed black polished hair and a white coat many sizes too big for him, looked inside George's mouth and exclaimed to the nurse that it was amazing that such an old man should have no fillings! I translated the doctor's words for George and the two of us tried not to laugh. George had a mouth full of false teeth!

The doctor then took George to a private area cordoned off by bed sheets. As he repeatedly whacked George's knee to test his reaction, George yelled to me in English, "Will you tell this clown that I haven't had a knee-jerk reaction since I was a kid?"

The trip into the city to get our photos taken was just as insane. Both sides of the street were being dug up to lay some pipes. I was worried that George might fall in. He was an intensely independent man, so I was trying to keep an eye on him without his realizing it. In the meantime I had lost the man from the university who had driven us in. While looking for him, I lost George who was walking ahead of us. I walked into several wrong buildings looking for the two of them.

Dodging bicycles and the hordes of people rushing to the market for food, I finally bumped into George. Together we found the building where we were to have our photos taken. The driver from the university was waiting there for us. We had lunch and got back to the university in time for the meeting with the two chairwomen and the curriculum director of the Foreign Languages Department.

The meeting with these three women topped off the first full day in China. They told me that I was scheduled to teach American literature to the juniors and seniors. My heart sank. Literature, more than the Bible, is where I find God most strongly connected to life. To teach literature would amount to being reminded of everything that I had come to Wuhan University of Technology to forget.

I was handed the two volumes of the literature textbooks, published in Shanghai, complete with Chinese footnotes. I glanced at the authors. The first volume included Washington Irving, Nathaniel Hawthorne, Mark Twain, Bret Harte, Stephen Crane, Jack London, O. Henry, and Ernest Hemingway—the usual choices for an anthology. Then I saw the authors in the second volume, and my heart sank again: Sherwood Anderson, F. Scott Fitzgerald, John Steinbeck, Irwin Shaw, Bernard Malamud, John Cheever, Saul Bellow, Flannery O'Connor, Joyce Carol Oates, and John Gardner. Old friends who had stoked the fires of my soul.

I felt like Dracula looking at the Cross. My reaction must have been obvious in my facial expression, because the curriculum director asked if I was displeased with the selection of stories. Her tone of voice indicated a sensitivity, perhaps even a fear that I didn't think much of their teaching material. I remember saying to her, "The selection of stories is excellent, but I didn't know I was supposed to teach American literature. Wouldn't the students benefit more if a Chinese faculty member taught them literature so that the deeper meanings could be explained in Chinese?"

She responded in a way that gave me face, saved her own, and made sure she would win: "We need an American expert to teach American literature so that our students can learn better."

My resistance was showing. George looked over the rim of his glasses and said to me under his breath, "Take it." I accepted the courses assigned me: two conversation classes for freshmen, conversation and writing classes for sophomores, and American literature classes for juniors and seniors.

Before the meeting ended, the curriculum director told me that the juniors and seniors had already completed the first volume of the literature texts. "So," she said with bright eyes and hunched up shoulders, "why don't you begin with the last story of the second volume?" Her suggestion made no sense. I figured it was just a "cute" idea. I nodded and glanced at the table of contents to find the last story of volume two. It was John Gardner's "Redemption."

Redemption

Classes were scheduled to begin in two days. My first class was writing with the sophomores and, the same morning, American literature with the seniors. I had no idea how to approach the writing class, so I sat on the sofa in my apartment on the evening of my first full day in Wuhan and began reading "Redemption." Something began to happen as I read:

> One day in April—a clear, blue day when there were crocuses in bloom—Jack Hawthorne ran over and killed his brother, David. Even at the last moment he could have

prevented his brother's death by slamming on the tractor
brakes, easily in reach for all the shortness of his legs;
but he was unable to think, or, rather, thought unclearly,
and so watched it happen, as he would again and again
watch it happen in his mind, with nearly undiminished
intensity and clarity, all his life.[2]

It was the stark contrast between the first and second halves
of Gardner's first sentence that caught my attention. He had captured in words a feeling I had had inside since my father's death
and my sister's diagnosis: the difference between "before and
after" the moment my father died—the difference between "before and after" my sister telephoned to tell me she had cancer. I
experienced again a sense of shock at the unfairness of life. This
was slap-in-the-face reality: the difference between the clear, blue
April day with crocuses in bloom—the onset of spring after the
long, cold, gray winter—and twelve-year-old Jack Hawthorne ac-
cidentally running over and killing his seven-year-old brother
David with a tractor.

The story pierced my heart as I read on through that hot,
humid early September evening in Wuhan, my hoped-for haven of
escape. I felt something for Jack Hawthorne. Maybe it was easier
to feel something for a character on a page in a story than for another human being. But I know I felt something for him. A barrier
was let down or at least acknowledged. I wanted to know how this
young boy went on living, how he perceived things after the stark
change in his life.

Jack Hawthorne was consumed with self-hatred as he lived
through the months after his brother's accidental death. He saw
his family and his life changed so drastically as to never be the
same again:

The damage to young Jack Hawthorne took a long while
healing...he had all the time in the world to cry and
swear bitterly at himself...He'd never loved his brother,
he raged out loud, never loved anyone as well as he
should have. He was incapable of love, he told himself
...He was inherently bad, a spiritual defective. He was

evil. Tears no longer came, though the storm went on building...The foulness of his nature became clearer and clearer in his mind until, like his father, he began to toy—dully but in morbid earnestness now—with the idea of suicide...he kept aloof...fists clenched, he raged inside his mind, grinding his teeth to drive out thought, at war with the universe.

Jack's father, Dale, was nearly destroyed by the death of his younger son, David. After the accident, his "mind swung violently...reversing itself almost hour by hour, from desperate faith to the most savage, black-hearted atheism." Dale Hawthorne started chain-smoking Lucky Strikes, and sometimes "he would forget for a while by abandoning reason and sensibility for love affairs." He'd leave the family for days at a time.

No one complained, at least not openly. A stranger might have condemned him, but no one in the family did, certainly not Jack, not even Jack's mother, though her sorrow was increased. Dale Hawthorne had always been, before the accident, a faithful man, one of the most fair-minded, genial farmers in the county. No one asked that, changed as he was, he do more for the moment, than survive.

Before the accident, Jack's mother had been a cheerful woman; she laughed often and loved telling stories. But after the accident, she cried at night and "did only as much as she had strength to do—so sapped by grief that she could barely move her arms." She would comfort Jack and his five-year-old sister Phoebe who had witnessed the accident while riding on the fender of the tractor Jack was driving. Mrs. Hawthorne would comfort her two remaining children and herself as well "by embracing them vehemently whenever new waves of guilt swept in, by constant reassurance and extravagant praise, frequent mention of how proud some relative would be" over her children's slightest accomplishments. She also forced on Jack and Phoebe comforts more permanent—piano lessons for Phoebe and French horn lessons for Jack. Mrs. Hawthorne kept herself busy with an

... endless, exhausting ritual of chores. Because she had,
at thirty-four, considerable strength of character—except
that, these days, she was always eating—and because,
also, she was a woman of strong religious faith, a woman
who, in her years of church work and teaching at the high
school, had made scores of close, for the most part equally religious, friends, with whom she regularly corre-
sponded, her letters, then theirs, half filling the mailbox
at the foot of the hill and cluttering every table, desk, and
niche in the large old house—friends who now frequently
visited or phoned—she was able to move step by step
past disaster and in the end keep her family from wreck.
She said very little to her children about her troubles. In
fact, except for the crying behind her closed door, she
kept her feelings strictly secret.

The detail of step-by-step feeling in the aftermath of the family's "before and after" the accident captivated me as I read that
night. While turning the pages, I found myself wanting ever more
eagerly to know how they would live through the changes. Once
in a while as I continued with my reading, I would recall that this
particular story had been selected to be read by Chinese students.
It was a reminder of the truth that this family's story is universal
in its realness.

Jack found moments of solace and peace with the animals
and in the early morning solitude on the farm. "He felt more community with the cows than with his uncles" who helped on the
farm. In the early morning, as the cows ate, Jack would

... listen to their chewing in the dark, close barn, a sound
as soothing, as infinitely restful, as waves along a shore,
and would feel their surprisingly warm, scented breath,
their bovine quiet, and for a while would find that his
anxiety had left him. With the cows, the barn cats, the
half-sleeping dog, he could forget and feel at home, feel
that life was pleasant. He felt the same when walking up
the long, fenced lane at the first light of sunrise—his
shoes and pants legs sopping wet with dew, his ears full
of birdcalls—going to bring in the herd from the upper

pasture. Sometimes on the way he would step off the deep, crooked cow path to pick cherries or red raspberries, brighter than jewels in the morning light. They were sweeter then than at any other time, and as he approached, clouds of sparrows would explode into flight from the branches, whirring off to safety. The whole countryside was sweet, early in the morning—newly cultivated corn to his left; to his right, alfalfa and, beyond that, wheat. He felt at one with it all. It was what life ought to be, what he'd once believed it was.

But he could not make such feelings last. *No,* he thought bitterly on one such morning, throwing stones at the dull, indifferent cows, driving them down the lane. However he might hate himself and all his race, a cow was no better, or a field of wheat.

Page by page, I was feeling more understanding and sympathy for Jack. I also found myself sensing that he was rapidly approaching the point of no return. I wondered if he might kill himself; his honesty seemed to leave him no escape.

The story progressed to a point a year and a half after the accident. It was August, and Jack was working in the field with the help of neighbors and cousins. His father had been gone for nearly three weeks this time. His sister Phoebe had brought out a basket lunch to those working in the field and found Jack sitting alone.

"It's chicken," she said, and smiled, kneeling. The basket was nearly as large as she was—Phoebe was seven—but she seemed to see nothing unreasonable in her having to lug it up the hill from the house. Her face was flushed, and drops of perspiration stood out along her hairline, but her smile was not only uncompromising but positively cheerful. The trip to the field was an escape from housework, he understood; even so, her happiness offended him.

As Phoebe took the food out of the basket, Jack thought her actions were similar to those of a child playing house. She pulled out a small plastic thermos of iced tea. "She looked up at him now.

'I brought you a thermos all for yourself because you always sit alone.' He softened a little without meaning to. 'Thanks,' he said."

The scene between Jack and Phoebe reminded me of my younger sister. Jack's attention to his sister was loving, despite his wanting to remain closed.

> She looked down again, and for all his self-absorption he was touched, noticing that she bowed her head in a way a much older girl might do, troubled by thought, though her not quite clean, dimpled hands were a child's. He saw that there was something she wanted to say and, to forestall it, brushed flying ants from the top of the thermos, unscrewed the cap, and poured himself iced tea...Jack drained the cup, brooding on his aching muscles.
>
> "Jack," his sister said, "did you want to say grace?"
>
> "Not really," he said, and glanced at her.
>
> He saw that she was looking at his face in alarm, her mouth slightly opened, eyes wide, growing wider, and though he didn't know why, his heart gave a jump. "I already said it," he mumbled. "Just not out loud."
>
> "Oh," she said, then smiled.

Phoebe was surviving in her own way; despite his self-absorbing self-hatred, Jack was touched by her honesty. He saw in her something that combined interrupted innocence and childlike openness. She deserved his respect.

> When everyone had finished eating she put the empty papers, the jug, and the smaller thermos in the basket, grinned at them all and said goodbye—whatever had bothered her was forgotten as soon as that—and, leaning far over, balancing the lightened but still-awkward basket, started across the stubble for the house. As he cranked the tractor she turned around to look back at them and wave. He nodded and, as if embarrassed, touched his straw hat.
>
> Not till he was doing the chores that night did he grasp what her look of alarm had meant. If he wouldn't

say grace, then perhaps there was no heaven. Their father would never get well, and David was dead. He squatted, drained of all strength again...

Phoebe touched Jack by her straightforwardness. The scene reveals how everyday life and a simple encounter with a loved one's openness can momentarily weave a connection.

Jack's father returned home after his three-week sojourn. The night he returned, Jack's emotions were, as usual, not in sync with the occasion, but honest:

"Hi, Dad," he brought out, and somehow managed to go to him and get down on his knees beside him and put his arm around his back. He felt dizzy now, nauseated, and he was crying like his father. "I hate you," he whispered too softly for any of them to hear.

Dale Hawthorne stayed home. "He worked long days, in control once more, though occasionally he smoked, pacing in his room nights, or rode off on his motorcycle for an hour or two, and seldom smiled." Jack was keeping silent now, "more private than before" his father's return. Having played the French horn almost since the time of the accident, he found in the horn his escape. "At night he'd go out to the cavernous haymow or up into the orchard and practice his French horn. One of these days, he told himself, they'd wake up and find him gone." Jack needed to be away from the herding warmth of his family; the horn was his excuse and his escape.

Those around him were conscious enough of what was happening—his parents and Phoebe, his uncles, aunts, and cousins, his mother's many friends. But there was nothing they could do. "That horn's his whole world," his mother often said, smiling but clasping her hands together. Soon he was playing third horn with the Batavia Civic Orchestra... He began riding the Bluebus to Rochester, Saturdays, to take lessons from Arcady Yegudkin, "the General," at the Eastman School of Music.

Gardner's description of Yegudkin is bizarre enough to suggest that he was a man who could be Jack's salvation. Someone as marginal as Yegudkin could break through Jack's year-and-a-half wall of self-hatred and aloofness. I myself found in Yegudkin a pivot, a reference point, to which I would return again and again as my three years in China progressed. With brutal honesty, the man lived unselfconsciously between two worlds. Gardner's grace with words prepared me, in some strange way, to meet Yegudkin.

> Yegudkin was seventy. He'd played principal horn in the orchestra of Czar Nikolai and at the time of the Revolution had escaped, with his wife, in a dramatic way. At the time of their purge of Kerenskyites, the Bolsheviks had loaded Yegudkin and his wife, along with hundreds more, onto railroad flatcars, reportedly to carry them to Siberia. In a desolate place, machine guns opened fire on the people on the flatcars, then soldiers pushed the bodies into a ravine, and the train moved on. The soldiers were not careful to see that everyone was dead. Perhaps they did not relish their work; in any case, they must have believed that, in a place so remote, a wounded survivor would have no chance against wolves and cold weather. The General and his wife were among the few who lived, he virtually unmarked, she horribly crippled. Local peasants nursed the few survivors back to health, and in time the Yegudkins escaped to Europe. There Yegudkin played horn with all the great orchestras and received such praise—so he claimed, spreading out his clippings—as no other master of French horn had received in all history. He would beam as he said it, his Tartar eyes flashing, and his smile was like a thrown-down gauntlet.

Of course there was no way of knowing how accurately Yegudkin's history presaged what was to happen in China at Tiananmen Square less than a year's time from that September night. That night what captured my interest was wanting to know what would happen to Jack and what role Yegudkin would play. I, too—in different ways and for different reasons—felt caught between two worlds: innocence and disillusionment, life and death, rawness and the denial of it, seeking and cynicism, what ought to be and what is. I wanted Gardner to give me some help, some way to follow. First, though, Yegudkin's rage set the stage:

> When it was time to give Jack's lip a rest, the General would speak earnestly, with the same energy he put into his singing, of the United States and his beloved Russia that he would nevermore see. The world was at that time filled with Russophobes. Yegudkin, whenever he read a paper, would be so enraged he could barely contain himself. "In all my age," he often said, furiously gesturing with his black cigar, "if the Russians would come to this country of America, I would take up a rifle and shot at them—*boof!* But the newspapers telling you lies, all lies! You think them dumb fools, these Russians? You think they are big, fat bush-overs?" He spoke of mile-long parades of weaponry, spoke of Russian cunning, spoke with great scorn, a sudden booming laugh, of Napoleon. Jack agreed with a nod to whatever the General said. Nevertheless, the old man roared on, taking great pleasure in his rage, it seemed, sometimes talking like a rabid communist, sometimes like a fascist, sometimes like a citizen helplessly caught between mindless, grinding forces, vast, idiot herds. The truth was, he hated both Russians and Americans about equally, cared only for music, his students and, possibly, his wife.

Yegudkin was a misfit "caught between mindless, grinding forces, vast, idiot herds"; Jack was a misfit trapped between wanting to live yet feeling unworthy. And my misfitness, acknowledged at that time, was provoked by death, death threatened, and feeling I didn't belong. The melding of the misfitness among the three of us was, I think, what held me bound to the story that night. It was an instinctive, unconscious, and unwilling connection. I understood Jack's aloofness. He used the French horn to escape; I used my missionary vocation. Both of us were waiting upon Yegudkin's eccentricity to give us some way of trying to continue.

Propelled into a Roofless Universe:
A Prospect both Liberating and Terrifying

A dear friend gave me a review of the Irish poet Seamus Heaney's book, *Seeing Things*. He thought the following passage would appeal to me. I can see now that Heaney describes what I had been feeling that night, and, like Gardner's story, Heaney's description gave me permission to go further:

> ... "would" is a favorite Heaney auxiliary verb, announcing an intention consigned to an indefinite future. What might come from such a discipline? A newfound voice from an exhausted spring? In any case it would be a baptism peculiarly his own.
>
> *Seeing Things*, Heaney's second collection of new poems ... continues to provide new answers to those questions, but, as we might expect, they are elliptical and aslant, teasing us *into* thought. Many of the poems celebrate his father whose death, he said in Kilkenny, propelled him into a whole new awareness of adulthood as life in a roofless universe, a prospect both liberating and terrifying.[3]

Yegudkin had lived with the terrifying and liberating awareness of adulthood opened up to him through violence and death. For Jack and for me, the roofless universe was only terrifying; we did not have Yegudkin's full awareness of the terror coupled with liberty. We were trying to build artificial roofs of protection against the terror created by death. I was at the time not able to perceive any liberating prospect because my terror hadn't found a way into the opening. Yegudkin revealed to me the way through terror to the liberating prospect into which death and suffering can propel one:

> One day a new horn he'd ordered from Germany, an Alexander, arrived at his office—a horn he'd gotten for a graduate student. The old man unwrapped and assembled it, the graduate student looking on—a shy young man,

blond, in a limp gray sweater—and the glint in the General's eye was like madness or at any rate lust, perhaps gluttony. When the horn was ready he went to the desk where he kept his clippings, his tools for the cleaning and repair of French horns, his cigars, photographs, and medals from the Czar, and pulled open a wide, shallow drawer. It contained perhaps a hundred mouthpieces, of all sizes and materials, from raw brass to lucite, silver, and gold, from the shallowest possible cup to the deepest. He selected one, fitted it into the horn, pressed the rim of the bell into the right side of his large belly—the horn seemed now as much a part of him as his arm or leg—clicked the shining keys to get the feel of them, then played. In that large, cork-lined room, it was as if, suddenly, a creature from some other universe had appeared, some realm where feelings become birds and dark sky, and spirit is more solid than stone. The sound was not so much loud as large, too large for a hundred French horns, it seemed. He began to play now not single notes but, to Jack's astonishment, chords—two notes at a time, then three. He began to play runs. As if charged with life independent of the man, the horn sound fluttered and flew crazily, like an enormous trapped hawk hunting frantically for escape. It flew to the bottom of the lower register, the foundation concert F, and crashed below it, and on down and down, as if the horn in Yegudkin's hand had no bottom, then suddenly changed its mind and flew upward in a split-second run to the horn's top E, dropped back to the middle and then ran once more, more fiercely at the E, and this time burst through it and fluttered, manic, in the trumpet range, then lightly dropped back into its own home range and, abruptly, in the middle of a note, stopped. The room still rang, shimmered like a vision.

"Good horn," said Yegudkin, and held the horn toward the graduate student, who sat, hands clamped on his knees, as if in a daze.

Jack Hawthorne stared at the instrument suspended in space and at his teacher's hairy hands. Before stopping to think, he said, "You think I'll ever play like that?"

Yegudkin laughed loudly, his black eyes widening, and it seemed that he grew larger, beatific and demonic at once, like the music; overwhelming. "Play like *me?*" he exclaimed.

I could hardly believe what I'd read. Gardner's words themselves were like "an enormous trapped hawk hunting frantically for escape." I experienced them that way because they reached down to the depths of what I had been feeling the past year of my life. Gardner's words plumbed, punctured, and took something with them out of my soul and into the air.

I know this may sound dramatic, but on my first full night in humid, hot Wuhan, I started crying. Not for my father or for the abrupt changes in my own life. There was a connection with the tears of the past year, but this went beyond that into "something" else. I wasn't sure of what at the time. I just knew that my own depths of terror had not been plumbed until I read Gardner's words describing the horn in Yegudkin's artistic hands—the spirit he gave the French horn.

I am reminded of Tracy's description of the artist quoted in Chapter 1. After observing that the difference between the artist and the rest of us is simply one of degree, Tracy points out that the artist is willing to undertake a "journey of intensification, a journey which most of us fear yet desire, shun yet demand." He goes on to note that "The journey into particularity in all its finitude and all its strivings for the infinite in this particular history in all its effects, personal and cultural, will with the artist be radically embraced."[4]

Yegudkin took the journey of intensification which Jack and I had shunned up to that point. The fear and desire meet in all people, yet the artist and the saint embrace their striving for the infinite in the particularity of their finiteness. Yegudkin's embrace of the French horn "seemed as much a part of him as his arm or leg." In this particularity, the demonic and the beatific lived together. The intensified journey was for Yegudkin not a denial but rather an invitation offered and accepted. Jack would embrace his horn and music by the story's end; I would embrace my missionary vocation, with time. Our escapes were transformed into our openings into the transcendent. Spirits more solid than stone. "Play like me?" Only if the terrifying and liberating prospects can together be accepted in the roofless universe.

Gardner's story concludes with Jack responding to Yegudkin's exclamation:

> Jack blinked, startled by the bluntness of the thing, the terrible lack of malice, and the truth of it. His face tingled and his legs went weak, as if the life were rushing out of them. He longed to be away from there, far away, safe. Perhaps Yegudkin sensed it. He turned gruff, sending away the graduate student, then finishing up the lesson. He said nothing, today, of the stupidity of mankind. When the lesson was over he saw Jack to the door and bid him goodbye... "Next Saturday?" he said, as if there might be some doubt.
>
> Jack nodded, blushing.
>
> At the door opening on the street he began to breathe more easily, though he was weeping. He set down the horn case to brush away his tears. The sidewalk was crowded—dazed-looking Saturday morning shoppers herding along irritably, meekly, through painfully bright light. Again he brushed tears away. He'd be late for his bus. Then the crowd opened for him and, with the horn cradled under his right arm, his music under his left, he plunged in, starting home.

Gardner's conclusion was prophetic for me. Jack's blinking at Yegudkin's exclamation—the bluntness, the terrible lack of malice, and the truth of it—startled him, woke him up. He wanted to be far away and safe. There is no safety save the acceptance of the truth. To deny this truth where the demonic and beatific find their home is to betray one's self. To accept this truth is to live in the openness of the roofless universe of true adulthood.

Gardner answers the how of approaching true adulthood, yet his answers are elliptical and aslant; and they tease us into thought. Gardner's words suggest the roofless universe: "the door opening," "breathe more easily," "weeping," "brush away," "painfully bright light," "the crowd opened for him," "he plunged in," "starting home." All these phrases bespeak Jack's emergence through the wall of aloofness and separation he'd constructed over the year and a half since the accident. His "before and after" delineation of time was brushed away as he began to live with the prospect of both the terrifying and the liberating awareness of adulthood.

For myself, I felt that night some sense of release through my connection with Gardner's characters. Jack cradled the horn under his right arm. The act of "cradling" is tender, life-giving, and nurturing. So, too, is the new awareness of adulthood in a roofless universe. Acceptance of the two-sided prospect, terrifying and liberating, needs acknowledgement, understanding, honesty, integrity, encouragement, and time. I found all of these qualities in Gardner that night. I would find all of them, and their antitheses, in China over the next three years. Challenges and attempts to bury the truth would, with time, serve only to strengthen the need for the two-sided prospect.

But that was for later. What I felt that early September night was the sort of strength that comes from seeing the clarity of the truth. It was as simple as that. And, in seeing it, some focus or transformation occurred. I suppose the energy I had been using to keep myself living blocked off from the truth had now shifted toward wanting to embrace it or needing to use it, *to live*. I wasn't fully conscious of it at the time, but I remember feeling something that enlivened me. Perhaps it was the release of tears. Or perhaps it was knowing the truth of Yegudkin's response to Jack's question, "Play like me?" Jack's "plunging in" toward home triggered this shift.

I wonder what I would have felt had I read "Redemption" in the States. I doubt if the impact of its clarity and truth would have been as piercing. There are escapes in one's home culture that simply aren't available in a foreign culture. Without those escapes, clarity of insight is more possible, honesty is more at hand. Gardner's words had evoked my latent honesty.

After savoring the story, I realized that I had classes to prepare. I didn't know where to begin, but I knew I was ready! I had not as yet even met the students I would teach that year, but I knew how I wanted to approach the American literature class. I would weave the stories through the themes of love and death. Something felt good about that as I went to bed that night. Jack

Hawthorne and Yegudkin had, through Gardner, begun the connection within myself that would lead me to connect with the students I would soon meet.

Plunging in with a Red Shirt

My first day of classes was filled with anxiety. I had two hours of the writing class with the sophomores to be followed by two hours of American literature with the seniors. I had already decided that I would use what had touched me in "Redemption" with the writing class. Of course I couldn't teach thematically in that class, but I had learned from experience what a writer can evoke in the reader. I wanted to try to communicate that to these students of writing. The attraction of grammar, spelling, and all things technical that had originally drawn me to China had vanished. I wanted to communicate with these people.

I wore a loose red shirt the first day of classes. It was hot and humid, so I had chosen a shirt that was comfortable and would let in some air. Time and again during my three years in Wuhan and even in letters I received from my former students after I left, I heard about that red shirt I wore for the first day of classes.

I was sweating like a field hand when I arrived at 7:45 A.M. for the 8:00 A.M. class. The thirty sophomores were all there on time, chatting away as they looked me over. The bell rang, and there was total silence. I began to introduce myself. I told them my father's parents had been born in Lebanon and my mother's in Italy. I told them I had grown up in the United States, first in an Italian ghetto and then in a Lebanese ghetto before our family moved out to the country when I was seven. I told them my father had died the previous year and that my mother had moved to a new apartment and was very active with the senior citizens' organization. I told them my older sister was married with two children and that she had cancer but was now healing. I told them my younger sister was a sculptor who taught at a university.

I was still sweating; it was dripping off my nose. "Nothing like calling attention to my nose," I thought. I knew that Chinese people marvel at foreigners' long noses and refer to us as "long noses"—either in derision or affection, depending on the relationship. I decided to ask them why they thought I was sweating so much. They all said it was because of the weather. I told them it was because I was nervous about meeting them. They all laughed. They were not accustomed to a teacher making fun of himself. I felt good.

I asked them to tell me their names and to say something about themselves. Because they were all English majors in the Foreign Languages Department, they had each either chosen or been given English names. I memorized their names through associations I made with the first impression I had of each of them. They were impressed by that.

After they had introduced themselves, I asked if they had any questions about me. "Why aren't you married?" I told them that people marry later in life in the States. (Because of the political situation, George and I could not speak openly about religion or the fact that we were priests. I had mentioned to George that in my resume I listed my master of divinity degree and included the fact that I was an ordained Roman Catholic priest. I also told him that the envelope of the July 6th letter of invitation had been addressed to me as "The Reverend Lawrence Lewis." We had no way of knowing if this was intentional. We decided that if anyone should ask if we were priests, we would not deny it, but would explain that we had been hired as English teachers and that was our work. George and I also decided that we would not celebrate Mass together; each of us celebrated separately in our apartments.)

The students went on to ask what I had studied in school. I told them I had studied sociology and then, in graduate school, psychological counseling. I explained that my doctorate was in the science of human formation, a new field that included study of spirituality, literature, psychology, and philosophy for the sake of understanding how certain experiences influence our lives. They asked what experience I had researched. I told them "waiting." They were surprised that I would write about something so boring. I was impressed by their responses and their English language ability.

One of the students said that the co-chair of the department had told them that if they had any questions about theology, they should ask either George or myself. I was taken aback by this!

They asked if I had studied theology. I answered that I had and that if any questions about theology came up we could discuss them. I was a little jittery about the theology issue, so I diverted the line of questions by telling them that George had been my sociology teacher in college. They were thrilled by the fact that we were together teaching in China.

After the long introduction, I described the course plan and grading system. I would assign a 100-150 word composition on a specific topic each week. I'd go over it, grading on content, style, and grammar, and give it back to them the following week. They groaned, but I assured them that the only way to learn writing in a foreign language is to write.

I then started discussing what makes a person a good writer. Before I left New York for China, one of our missioners had suggested that I take some books with me—anthologies of poetry, conversation texts, stories, etc. One of the paperbacks I had brought was *Immortal Poems of the English Language*. The day before classes had begun, I had read the Introduction by Oscar Williams. I wrote on the blackboard that morning: "Anyone who knows how to love, or to suffer, or to think, anyone who wishes to live fully, needs and seeks poetry."[5]

I had also brought with me a page from a magazine depicting Georgia O'Keeffe's "Red Poppy" with her words printed above the painting. I passed around the page and wrote O'Keeffe's words on the blackboard:

Still—in a way—nobody sees a flower—really—
it is so small—we haven't time—
and to see takes time, like to have a friend takes time.

I tried to explain to the students that a good writer or artist perceives things differently or at least with more care than most other people. I knew I was dealing with content that could be difficult for them to comprehend. Since English was not their first language, I said similar things in different ways to get my point across. In my enthusiasm for what had fired me up, I wanted to be as certain as possible that they understood what I was saying.

From the looks on their faces I could tell that the students had grasped what I was trying to say. I went on to tell them that I would be asking them, sometime during this semester, to write a poem. They groaned again. I assured them that a good poem communicates something very simply and directly. I wasn't looking for some strictly disciplined style of poetry writing. I wanted them to write a poem because I thought it would help train their way of seeing. I told them I wanted them to dig into themselves and put their thoughts on paper.

We then had a ten-minute break. The bell rang at full throttle for a full fifteen seconds—a sound I never got used to, even after three years. As soon as the bell rang, I went out into the corridor and lit up a cigarette. I was smoking a Chinese brand that I had bought at the campus store the day before. I offered one to a student. He told me that I was smoking a poor brand and that he would bring a better brand to my apartment. In the corridor I chatted with the students in Chinese. (In class I always spoke English.) I heard my students telling students from other classes that I could speak Chinese. When they asked where I had learned it, I told them I had been in Taiwan and studied the language there.

As the second hour of class began, I asked if they had any questions. First, they wanted clarification on the grading system. Then they wanted to know what the topic for the first composition would be. After explaining the grading system, I said that for next week I wanted them to write about one object in nature. They were to write about what the object looked like and reminded them of; its colors and smells; how it blew in the breeze; memories it had for them. They looked at me as if I had come from Mars, not the States.

I then held up a piece of chalk and asked them to talk about it. I wrote their responses on the blackboard: white, dusty, long, a teacher uses it, breaks easily, used on the blackboard. I asked them to think about the first time they had used a piece of chalk. Were they in primary school? Were they afraid of the teacher? Were they embarrassed when the teacher asked them to go to the blackboard and write? Were they homesick for their childhood days? Were they glad they were no longer children? I saw that they were catching on to the first assignment.

We concluded the first class with the following words of Dag Hammarskjold, who had been Secretary General of the United Nations: "Let me read with open eyes the book my days are writing—and learn."[6] I summarized the day's class by reminding the students that good writing depends on how well they observe and reflect upon their lives. My first class in China ended with the fifteen-second ringing of the bell.

As I stood out in the corridor having another cigarette, I heard the students greeting each other after the summer vacation and talking together. "The new foreign teacher speaks Chinese...he smokes bad Chinese cigarettes...he lived in Taiwan...he welcomed us to visit his apartment...the old man is his teacher from college." A group gathered around me, and we talked. They were bright, friendly, inquisitive.

After the twenty-minute break between the two morning classes, I went into the senior American literature classroom. Again, I started sweating. There were thirty-four seniors, a fifty/fifty ratio of male and female—quite different from the six-male sophomore class. I introduced myself to the seniors, telling them the same things I had told the sophomores. When they introduced themselves, I was again impressed by their English ability. I praised them and asked how their English had become so good. They responded by saying that they had had dedicated and hard-working middle school teachers. I told them that I knew they were dedicated too.

It was then time to move into the subject matter of the course. I was nervous, but still fired by Gardner's characters. I began by stating my opinion that all great world literature is concerned with love and death—that nothing changes our lives or shapes the world as much as do love and death. The students did not immediately agree; heads tilted questioningly and some eyebrows were raised.

I then asked the students to recall their favorite works of literature—either Chinese or English. I asked them to think about why they remembered these particular works. What was happening in their lives when they read these works? How did reading these pieces of literature affect their lives at the time? As I asked these questions, I could see that the expressions on the students' faces were quite serious. I suggested that they take time to write down somewhere the titles of the works they were now remembering. I then said I would bet them that what they were remembering was, in one form or another, concerned with either love or death.

I explained that what I meant by death was not necessarily biological death, but death in all its various forms: weakness, failure, loneliness, anxiety, fear, rejection, despair—anything that seems to prevent us from living life as completely as possible or that "stops" the flow of our lives. Similarly, I explained that what I meant by love was not necessarily romantic love, but love in all its forms: joy, friendship, compassion, sacrifice, encouragement, hope—anything that gives life to and supports the human spirit and understanding among people.

I then heard myself describing how my father's death and my sister's cancer had stopped my life—how these events had caused my family to question the meaning of life. I heard myself describing how, when these things happened, I found myself not caring about anything, how I was afraid of almost everything; how the most simple things in my life could cause me to feel tremendous despair or tremendous hope; and how I hadn't usually paid that much attention to these things before.

I remember feeling, as I talked, that it was a little strange to be saying these things to students I had just met. I watched their reactions: some lowered their heads, some stared at me, some blushed. I went on to say that loved ones become more precious to us at times when death or the threat of death surrounds us. I said that loved ones and friends cannot take away our pain, but they can understand us and that is what we need most.

Then I asked them to open the second volume of their literature texts to the last story, "Redemption." I wrote the definition of *redemption* on the blackboard: "to obtain the release of; to set free or save." I suggested that this story was about Jack being released from something, about his being saved. After we read the first line of the story, I spent a great deal of time talking about the stark contrast, the slap-in-the-face moment that separated young Jack's life into "before" and "after." I found phrases that described the lives of Jack's father and mother before and after the death of their son. I wrote the important words on the blackboard. The bell announced the end of the first hour.

Before I could get out the door for a cigarette, one of the students came up to me and said, "I am sorry for the death of your father. I hope health for your sister." Immediately, tears came to my eyes. I thanked her. Her words split open my heart. I remember feeling it was as if she had been the first person to express such direct sympathy and good wishes.

After the class break I emphasized how literature can be both a tremendous teacher and a support in life. I wrote the Williams and Hammarskjold quotations on the board in this class also. We then looked briefly at the characters in "Redemption," and I asked them to read the story for the next class. To help them understand the story in a more personal manner, I asked them to write a letter to one of the characters in the story. I suggested that they write to that person as if he or she were a friend. They were to bring the letter to the next class.

Surrounded by Grace

My first day of classes had ended. I was elated, relieved, and exhausted. I was also astonished at the sudden transformation called forth by Gardner's "Redemption."

At supper that night George and I discussed the day's classes. He was teaching English conversation and a course in American history/sociology. Both of us were amazed at the quality of our students' English.

Over supper, we also planned the schedule of the Thursday night "American Culture Talks" that were part of our contract. George explained that almost every Chinese university with foreign teachers sponsored talks like these. They were open to the entire university as well as to other schools in the area. George and I would alternate weeks, as we were the only two foreign teachers at the university that year. George was familiar with the talks since he had given them at the other two universities where he'd taught. He usually spoke about some historical event, such as the Industrial Revolution, or about things such as inventions, the election process, etc. I told him that for my first talk I would be interested in presenting something on the American family system and how it has changed over the generations. He thought that sounded all right. He said he would take the first Thursday. I thanked him and said I'd attend his talk to get an idea of how they are conducted.

George said, "No, you can't."

I asked, "Why? Does the university object to having a foreign teacher attend the lectures of another? Is it some rule they have?"

George replied, "No. *I* don't want you there."

I was puzzled and laughed spontaneously, half-thinking George was joking and half-feeling almost hurt at his response. I said, "What?"

"I don't want you there. I'd feel threatened." He stated this matter-of-factly without looking up from his food.

I said, "But, George, I know nothing about American history."

"I'd feel threatened with you in the room," he responded. I knew that was the end of the conversation. We finished supper and went for a walk around campus.

When I got back to my apartment and thought about what George had said at supper, I felt a tenderness for him. George was a man of vast intelligence, with rich and varied experience. He never flaunted his knowledge. He was a man of integrity, with an eye for quality in people and things. He was also a person who went quietly out of his way for his friends. I remember thinking that night that here was a seventy-nine-year-old man who was still young enough in his mind and heart to feel threatened by a person half his age who couldn't possibly match his intelligence. And that he could tell me so matter-of-factly why he didn't want me attending his lecture!

As I got to know George over our year together, I began to see that what he had said that night revealed more about him than I'd realized at the time. I knew he balked at the soul-baring tactics of recent seminary formation that attempted to help people understand themselves and others. He felt that it was based on forced friendships that reduced people to tools for themselves and others. He had discussed this with me. What he'd told me that night at supper was a fact, pure and simple, from an honest, tender-hearted man. I felt trusted by him.

As I ended that day, I felt surrounded by graces: George's directness, Gardner's honesty in Jack and Yegudkin, and the students' openness. I felt silently blessed.

The following week in class confirmed the silent sense of grace I was feeling. I had given the sophomores, juniors, and seniors selections from William Faulkner's "Address Upon Receiving the Nobel Prize for Literature." I wanted to convey to them the power, responsibility and, as Faulkner says, the privilege of the writer. Faulkner's speech touched me in its straight-on poetry:

> Our tragedy today is a general and universal physical fear so long sustained by now that we can even bear it. There are no longer problems of the spirit. There is only the question: When will I be blown up? Because of this, the young man or woman writing today has forgotten the problems of the human heart in conflict with itself which alone can make good writing because only that is worth writing about, worth the agony and the sweat.
>
> He must learn them again. He must teach himself that the basest of all things is to be afraid; and, teaching himself that, forget it forever, leaving no room in his workshop for anything but the old verities and truths of the heart, the old universal truths lacking which any story is ephemeral and doomed—love and honor and pity and pride and compassion and sacrifice. Until he does so, he labors under a curse. He writes not of love but of lust, of defeats in which nobody loses anything of value, of victories without hope and, worst of all, without pity or compassion. His griefs grieve on no universal bones, leaving no scars. He writes not of the heart but of the glands.
>
> Until he relearns these things, he will write as though he stood among and watched the end of man. I decline to accept the end of man. It is easy enough to say that man is immortal simply because he will endure: that when the last ding-dong of doom has clanged and faded from the last worthless rock hanging tideless in the last red and dying evening, that even then there will still be one more sound: that of his puny inexhaustible voice, still talking. I refuse to accept this. I believe that man will not merely endure: he will prevail. He is immortal, not because he alone among creatures has an inexhaustible voice, but because he has a soul, a spirit capable of compassion and sacrifice and endurance. The poet's, the writer's, duty is to write about these things. It is his privilege to help man

endure by lifting his heart, by reminding him of the courage and honor and hope and pride and compassion and pity and sacrifice which have been the glory of his past. The poet's voice need not merely be the record of man, it can be one of the props, the pillars to help him endure and prevail.[7]

The students in the literature classes had seen how Gardner's characters fulfilled Faulkner's words. The letters that the juniors and seniors had written to the characters in "Redemption" revealed the connection between the story and their lives. Those in the writing class appreciated Faulkner's direction, but questioned their ability to follow such a call. They did, however, begin to think more carefully of what writing demanded of them. Their compositions indicated they were trying. I was more than pleased by the students' attention and response to the material.

As the days proceeded, I started sensing that the students felt they were being taken seriously. I knew from experience in Taiwan that children are the low ones on the totem pole of Chinese society. Often they live just to fulfill their parents' expectations. Also, there is such pressure to get into university that they have no time to think or to seriously develop their own thought.

I sensed that they knew I was expecting things of them, that I believed they had something to give. The long-nosed foreigner, the misfit, saw in them how their own misfitness could be a direct shunt to their souls. I took them seriously because I felt their frustration in not being taken seriously. It was something that went beneath and beyond mere social or cultural factors. At any rate, I felt a mutual energy being generated.

It was at about this time that I met Xie Lau Shi in our encounter on the grassy area during the morning class break. I recall thinking about her that afternoon as I was preparing classes for the next day. I was alone in my apartment when suddenly my eyes started burning. Tears appeared as I remembered her being laughed at by the students who had been there that morning. They had laughed at her craziness and they had laughed when I called her Teacher Xie. I knew they had laughed because they were embarrassed.

Yet there was something more to their laughter. She was an outsider. Immediately I felt a connection with something in her, a connection that was similar to what I felt was growing between myself and the students. We all, to one degree or another, were misfits. The students were not seen as individuals but rather as pawns to please others. Xie Lau Shi was "crazy." I was a long-nosed foreigner in China, and when in the States I was "out of the loop."

I suppose this realization made the students' laughter that morning all the more hurtful. It was as if their laughter had said, "She fits in even less than we do." She didn't deserve to be laughed at; no one does. Since we're all misfits, why laugh at each other?

Xie Lau Shi didn't reveal any of her hurt. Her twinkle-eyed smile seemed to indicate that she hadn't heard their laughter. But I knew she had, and I had. In a sense, I felt positioned between two sets of misfits: the students and people like Xie Lau Shi. I found that strange and, in a way, it made my own misfitness, in all its dimensions, all the more pronounced. I wasn't at all sure at the time what this realization would demand of me.

"Are you home?"

As the October 1st National Day long weekend holiday approached, I was looking forward to having a few days to think about all that had been happening. Moreover, the first anniversary of my father's death was that weekend. George was planning to fly to visit friends in the Southeast where he had taught for the previous two years. He graciously invited me to go, but I told him I wanted to stay home. He knew it was my father's anniversary. In his typically thoughtful fashion, he left a brief note at my door the morning he left.

On the Saturday evening of that weekend, there was a movie and a dance on campus. It was quite hot, so my windows were open wide to let in the breeze. I could hear music coming from one of the student dining halls where the dance was being held. Waltzes, disco music, and laughter could be heard all over the campus.

As I sat alone, reliving that day one year ago and all that had led to my father's death, I got an empty-stomach feeling. One month after my father had been diagnosed with cancer, he and my mother had driven to visit me at the apartment where I was living during my sabbatical. My father was coming out of an emotional slump, and the two of us had planned to go fishing.

While they were on their way, my older sister telephoned to say that she had just received a call from her doctor telling her she had been diagnosed with cancer. She had previously found a lump on her neck and had been told by several doctors it meant nothing. Being a nurse, she was planning to help care for my father when things grew worse. We all encouraged her to have the lump checked out. When she did, she was told a biopsy was needed but there was a 99 percent likelihood that the lump was benign. Oddly enough, we weren't worried. Then came her telephone call. I fell into the chair as I heard her sobbing, "I'm so afraid."

I thought to myself, "Dear God, what is happening?" This was devastating. I couldn't believe it. I kept her on the phone for a while and she told me that my brother-in-law was on his way home. He called when he arrived; the two of us agreed that I would make the decision as to whether to tell my parents or have them telephone my sister. I was numb.

I heard their car pull into the parking lot and went out to help them unpack. My father seemed to be in good spirits. He came in and sat down and I got him some sherbet. He was getting ready to turn on the television when I asked him to wait a bit and called my mother into the living room. I told them my sister had phoned and that the lump was malignant. My mother covered her face with her hands and, still standing, started rocking back and forth, crying, "What's happening to our family?" My father said, "I stopped praying too soon." Then, after the first shock waves had subsided, they called my sister and spoke with her.

All these memories were running through my mind in Wuhan, and I knew my mother and sisters were thinking about the same things at home. Details I had thought about over and over were recollected. My father and I did go fishing the next day. The two of us sat alone along the shore of a giant reservoir. It was a perfect day for fishing—on the brink of rain and quiet. He couldn't cast because he was too weak. After casting a few times, I sat down on a rock and looked over at him. "What's happening to us, Dad?"

"I can handle what's happening to me, but your sister..." He lapsed into silence. Then he said, "I've had one problem my whole life." When I asked him what it was, I was shocked to hear him say: "I've never been able to express my feelings." I'd have given my arms to hear those words twenty years earlier.

"We've learned to interpret your feelings, Dad. We know how you feel," I said. Then I added, "You've been a good father."

He looked at me from the rock he was sitting on. "Well, I can't say you've been a bad son. In fact, you've been perfect." We were saying all the things we wanted and needed to say. Finally he said, "What do you say we pack up this gear and go find us a gin mill?"

We packed up the fishing poles and worms and somehow found a beer joint. My father hadn't been able to drink beer since he had been diagnosed with cancer. It hadn't tasted good to him. We had a Miller's draft. It was ice cold. He smacked his lips and said, "That hits the spot." We had another and some beer nuts. It would be his last beer. We drove home with the windows wide open and stopped and got some cucumbers at a roadside vegetable stand. I thanked him when we got back to the apartment. I knew I would remember that day forever.

I recalled the last time I saw him at home. I tucked him into bed. He said as I kissed him goodnight in the dark, "Thanks for everything. I love you. You're a good boy." I knew he would soon die.

In the hospital he spiked a high fever. Together with the nurse, my mother, younger sister, and I gave him ice baths. He was so weak he couldn't talk. I told him it was a special situation, and I would give him absolution for all his past sins. He nodded his head, indicating that he understood. I said some prayers about God's mercy and then the prayer of absolution. As soon as I finished, he said, "Amen. Amen." Those were the last words I heard him say. I kissed his face and head before I left.

I wanted to be home now to visit those places, especially the reservoir and the beer joint. As I was thinking about his three days

in the hospital, I heard a voice, a small, almost gentle voice saying, "Larry?...Larry?...Are you home?" I realized the voice was
outside my window. As I looked out the window from the second
floor, I saw Eddie, a sophomore in the writing class. He looked up
and said again, "Are you home?"

I said, "Sure. I'll be right down to let you in."

As soon as he came in the door, he said, "I am lonely, so I
came to visit you." We sat and talked and drank tea for almost two
hours. He said my tea was all right, but that the tea from his home
province was the best in all China and he'd bring me some after
the Spring Festival holiday.

I asked Eddie about his family. He had two brothers and said
that he was the youngest and the first to attend university. He told
me his father had been killed suddenly in a truck accident a few
years ago. He talked freely, and I felt good that he was there. He
said that everything had changed in his family after his father's
sudden death. I couldn't wait until he was a junior and could read
the truth of Jack Hawthorne's life. As he left he thanked me for
the tea. I thanked him for coming and said it was very good for
me since this was the anniversary of my father's death. Eddie
smiled in understanding.

When I came back upstairs after seeing Eddie to the door, I
looked at my father's 8 x 10 photograph, the one we had placed
on his coffin. I looked at his warm smile and knew he would have
liked Eddie. During those years in China I would often glance
over the shoulder of the person I was talking with and see my father's photo. He would have liked it there; the people were down-
to-earth and took time to talk.

Concentrate on Creating the
Directness of One Emotion

After visiting with Eddie, I thought it was time to ask the sophomores to write a poem. Eddie had talked so openly that I wanted
to give the others a chance to express themselves freely too.

I had never forgotten a book by Kenneth Koch titled *I Never
Told Anybody: Teaching Poetry Writing in a Nursing Home*. Koch
documented how he had helped elderly people to remember their

past and their emotions through poetry writing. His efforts had enabled them to revive their memories and imaginations as well as to experience a sense of creating something beautiful.

The instruction he gave them was simple, and it helped them get in touch with interior feelings that perhaps had been long dormant. By reviving their imaginative skills, Koch helped them tap into their poetic nature and discover a new dimension in their lives. In one lesson Koch instructed them to call to mind one memory, associate it with a color, and write a poem.

As I prepared my sophomore students for this assignment, I used Koch's method and wrote on the blackboard the following poem by Mary Tkalec, an eighty-nine-year-old woman in Koch's class:

> I like green; I used to see so many greens on the farm.
> I used to wear green, and sometimes my mother couldn't
>   find me,
> Because I was green in the green.[8]

I told the sophomores to keep their poem simple and to use the poem to make the memory live through the color they chose. I also told them not to worry about the grammar, but to concentrate on creating the directness of one emotion through the memory. I knew this would be a difficult assignment, but I wanted them to try. I was also eager to read what they had to say. I had had enough glimmers to expect something good from them. They needed only the chance to express what was inside.

When I got their poems the following week, I was amazed. Eddie's poem, "Where is Green?" opens this chapter. I thought he had beautifully expressed the loss of innocence through which hope comes anew. He recalled his childhood sense of being surrounded by green. His expectations that green would remain everywhere with him were shattered, not only by the blatant losses of green through disease and war, but perhaps also by the more subtle and deadly losses through deception. His conclusion, "But for the peace of green I'm waiting," called out for my support. I could give it genuinely because I felt it through his poem.

There was another poem, written by Norie, that touched me. Her poem confirmed the truth that remembering is sacred:

"White Yulan"

Yulan magnolia in bloom—
White, white, white,
Broke my heart.
My mother lay still dressed in white.
With white Yulan flowers around her.
Teardrops dripped down on her dress.

Yulan magnolia in bloom—
White, white, white,
Broke my heart deeply.
Slowly my mother went to the holy place
Where she would sleep forever.
White paper flakes were flying
Just like Yulan flowers.

Yulan magnolia in bloom—
Pure, pure, pure,
Comforted my heart a little
I know:

My mother is living in heaven,
Leaving pure Yulan flowers in bloom,
Before me.
Pure and holy.
Pure and holy.

Eddie's poem had asked straightforwardly the question that most adults forget. His honesty in asking the question (especially in light of his father's death) and Norie's testimony to her mother led me further toward my own interior void, toward the roofless universe into which we are propelled. After only one and a half months, I felt I belonged in China. It was not because I fit in, but precisely because I did *not* that I felt at home. What these students were writing came from and through their felt misfitness and the void that brought it to light. Beginning with Gardner's characters, the way the Chinese students had responded to them, what these students were saying and writing in class, and how

Xie Lau Shi and George were living reminders of what honesty can be—I was learning again that social misfitness can be "greenless" or the doorway through which we can live life more to the full.

When I returned Norie's poem, I wrote her a note and asked for a copy of the poem. She wrote me the following letter on October 17, 1988:

Dear Sir:

Thanks for your letter. Words cannot sufficiently express the mixed sense of gratitude and sadness I felt on reading your letter. Tears couldn't help coming to my eyes, but I managed to hold them back, still smiling.

I cannot forget the first time that I met you. On hearing you lost your dear father, I was very sad and thought of my dead mother. I wanted to give you expressions of sympathy and have a heart-to-heart talk with you. But I didn't because I was too shy.

It's October now. In your hometown the autumn leaves are most beautiful. I think of your father as well as you. Your dear father is dead for a whole year. I want to know which day is the anniversary of your father's death. Can I commemorate him with you? According to Chinese custom, some commemorative activities should be held on the day of the death of a parent. Would you please give me a beautiful autumn leaf? I would like to share it with you to remember your dead father.

My mother was very kind. She was a good mother. I love her deeply. She died of terrible cancer in 1984. I will never forget her until my life stops. My mother's name was Yulan, and she liked Yulan flowers. In my opinion she is holy and pure like white Yulan. So I have Yulan flowers to remember my mother...I will copy down the poem for you. Dear Sir, you are very kind and respectable. I esteem you very much...

Yours respectfully,

Norie

As I sit here now surrounded by these poems and letters, I see that what I am writing reads like a story, almost like a fable. My journey to China, the people I met—it all seems like it was meant to be, it was more than just coincidence. Everything and everyone seem to have been taking me back to the very thing I had been trying to escape. I can see now that, essentially, I was afraid of being alive. This sounds as drastic as does the term misfit, but it is true. I went to China to forget. The people and situations there called me to remembrance.

They not only asked, "Where is green?" but they pointed me back to a place where I knew green had always been. I hadn't returned there in a long time. I had forgotten the joy and peace that is possible. I belonged there, and the people in China were asking me to return. I am not speaking metaphorically. There was a place I was being directed back to reclaim. I had found God there. It was a place where I fit in and which eventually led me to my vocation as a foreign missioner.

3

"... THE FOUNTAIN-LIGHT OF ALL OUR DAY"

Remembering Where

> But for those first affections,
> Those shadowy recollections,
> Which, be they what they may,
> Are yet the fountain-light of all our day,
> Are yet a master light of all our seeing;
> Uphold us, cherish, and have power to make
> Our noisy years seem moments in the being
> Of the eternal Silence: truths that wake,
> To perish never;
> Which neither listlessness, nor mad endeavor,
> Nor Man nor Boy,
> Nor all that is at enmity with joy,
> Can utterly abolish or destroy!
>
> William Wordsworth,
> "Ode on Intimations of Immortality"
> from *Recollections of Early Childhood*

From the earliest time I can remember until I was fourteen years old, I was a fat little child. Relatives found me "cute." I was ring-bearer for two of my cousins' weddings. The tuxedo was tailor-made. New clothes were always bought in the "huskies" department.

I didn't mind all this until our family moved to the country when I was seven. While I lived in the city, I wore sports jackets, bow ties, and short pants to school. Dressing like this in the country didn't work. The other children made fun of me—not just because of my clothes, but especially because of my fatness. They would taunt, "Here comes fatty! Make room for fatty," when our first-grade teacher would gather us around her for reading circle. I remember literally wedging myself into the circle on the floor.

I dreaded going to school, especially on gym days. I hated being made fun of and being laughed at. Because I was smart and had a good sense of humor, I could make the other children laugh. I felt that if I could make them laugh, they would like me. But I dreaded it all. I remember one day faking being sick so I wouldn't have to go to school. My father hadn't left for work yet, and he and my mother came into my bedroom. They wanted to know what was wrong. I didn't have a fever, and they were puzzled. I uncontrollably blubbered out, "They call me fatty!"

My parents tried to help. They took me to a doctor, and I was put on a diet: no bread and potatoes at the same meal and fewer sweets. My parents also got me my first pair of dungarees and a lunchbox similar to my father's. I felt so proud walking to school dressed like the other kids. Before arriving at school that morning, I tripped and fell on my new lunchbox, denting it and squashing the banana inside!

I also remember playing bush-league baseball one summer. I was, of course, on the worst team, the Cardinals. We wore yellow shirts with "Cardinals" written in red across the chest, tan pants, and red baseball hats. I was always put in center field so the right and left fielders could cover for me. One night our team was in the field so long that I wet my pants. It wouldn't have been too bad except for the tan pants. The stains went halfway down my pants' legs. Everyone in the bleachers and the other team members and even the Cardinals were pointing and laughing at me. I stayed there in center field, though. It seemed that nothing could take away my not fitting in. I longed for a place where I would not be laughed at.

The Rear, Right-hand Side Pew of St. Mary's

I found one. When I was eight or nine I started going to church every morning during Lent. We didn't have a Catholic school in our town when I was young, so no one forced, pressured, or even suggested that I attend Mass during Lent. I went on my own because I wanted to. Every day I would set off alone on the one-mile walk to church for the 7:30 Mass. I would sit by myself in the rear, right-hand side of St. Mary's, placing my school books, lunchbox, and whatever school project we were working on at the time next to me on the pew.

That pew was my home each morning. I loved the smells of the beeswax candles and the wooden pews. I loved the high ceiling and the stained-glass windows. When Mass ended, the images in those windows would begin to appear as the sun started shining through them. I felt at home. And I felt and I knew that God did not laugh at me. I don't know why I felt it, since no one had ever suggested it to me. People didn't talk about God's love in the mid-1950s. But *I* knew that God didn't laugh at people. I just knew it, and I felt it.

How I enjoyed that walk to Mass each morning. It was dark and quiet and the air smelled fresh. I could see people begin to turn on the lights in their homes. Sometimes there would be sudden snowstorms or rain or even ice storms. March weather is that way. Over the course of the forty days of Lent, hints of spring would appear.

Most of all, though, I loved going each day because I knew God did not laugh at me because I was fat. I never dreaded the Mass ending. I didn't feel that I wanted or needed to stay there forever. It wasn't a safe refuge or an escape. It was a special time for me each morning during Lent each year because I felt "not laughed at" by God. I suppose today we would say I felt accepted. But as a child of eight or nine I only knew God didn't laugh at me, and I felt so very good.

There were other children at school who were laughed at besides me. They were the ones from poor families. They were the "dumb" kids. They were the ones who stank because they were poor. They were the ones whose "germs" the "in-crowd" passed on with "no-returns" if one of these misfits happened to brush up against them. How cruel it was!

I felt bad for these others who were laughed at. They didn't have the good grades I had to appear acceptable. They couldn't muster the sense of humor I had to make others laugh with them. My social misfitness showed, as did theirs. But I had some resources and energy to fit in a little. It wasn't that I wanted to drag these other misfits to church with me. I just knew that things were not meant to be this way, that no one was meant to be laughed at. I knew then—maybe not consciously, but I knew—that someday and somehow I wanted to be someone whose job it was to let people know that God doesn't laugh at us. I didn't tell anyone about my aspirations then. I didn't tell anyone until I entered Maryknoll at the age of nineteen.

I got "thin" when I was fourteen. (I had had several bouts of strep throat throughout that year.) After becoming thin and looking as if I fit in, I both forgot and remembered my point of truth.

When I was eight years old, we had gotten "prayer-partners" in Sunday School. Mine was a Maryknoll priest, Father George Haggerty, M.M., who was working at the time in Taiwan. We children were supposed to say a particular prayer for these prayer-partners every Monday. I still have the prayer card with Our Lady of Maryknoll, surrounded by children of all nations on one side and the prayer on the other. I faithfully offered the prayer each Monday.

Father Haggerty and I would exchange letters three or four times a year. He never once even hinted at my becoming a priest. In his letters he would tell me about the Chinese people. His letters sparked in me a longing for adventure, and the feeling that I was different drew me to want to work outside my home culture, away from what was familiar. The fourteen years of being a fatty left their mark on my soul.

Originally, when I entered college, I had intended to enroll in a program that would train me to teach the mentally impaired. Then, somehow, I remembered what I had wanted so deeply to be. While I was trying to decide which group of priests to enter, the only thing I knew for sure was that I did not want to work in the United States. I wanted to join a group whose primary work was foreign mission. I entered Maryknoll as a college sophomore.

During my seminary education and formation, I was blessed every so often with priests and brothers whose outlooks on life and concern for people led me naturally into wholesome self-reflection. There were also opportunities for psychological counseling. I took advantage of these and, for the most part, found them helpful. After obtaining a master's degree in pastoral counseling, I worked as a pastoral counselor in Taiwan. My doctoral studies in spiritual formation also provided me with time and space to delve into my personal history with the guidance of a patient therapist.

Over the years, I've had time in conducive atmospheres to continue discovering how my past has affected my present life, my decisions and ways of perceiving in ways both positive and negative. I am, with the grace of God and hard work, learning how to live life more to the full. I have been blessed with friends of integrity whose lives naturally exemplify goodness.

I reflect often on my motivation for becoming a missionary priest and why I remain one. More than the theology studied, the spiritual direction received, the seminars attended, the degrees earned—all or most of them good in themselves—I know with every ounce of truth and conviction in me that attending those early morning Lenten Masses when I sat alone in the rear, right-hand side of St. Mary's was and continues to be my point of reference, motivation, and sustenance as a human, a priest, and a missioner. I felt like a misfit then and somehow I knew that Jesus was one too. He understood me, and I wanted others who didn't fit socially to know about him. Period.

What I am saying is that I have been able to delve with respect and support into my past and understand why I was a fat little child. Some form of deprivation, some threat, provoked my needing and trying to compensate or protect myself. I need not go into specifics here to illustrate the point.

Each person has his or her reason for being and feeling like a social misfit. Whatever the provocations, unique to each of our histories, were, and whatever we may do to understand them for the sake of trying to live life more freely and more fully, the fact remains that the years of feeling like a misfit leave their mark, their scars. It is up to each of us to work at trying to be more interiorly free with the remaining scars. We must learn to perceive and live with these scars as sacraments that reveal the void that brings us to the gateway where the God Who doesn't laugh at us awaits.

Even though I might look as if I fit in, I always feel fat whenever I see social misfits on the street—the blind, the elderly, the deaf, the "crazies."[1] And then I remember God's being with us, not laughing. I also remember God's way whenever I am backed against the wall. I feel fat again whenever I am under pressure or for some reason am not meeting some cultural norm or measuring up to what might be expected of me by others or by society in general. The fat feeling comes and right behind it are those Lenten morning Masses at St. Mary's.

This is my truth. No human being can take it away. No human being gave it to me. God did. Whoever would have thought my fatness would have become the sacrament that attracted and attracts me to God?

It is as simple and as complex as that. I was drawn to God through the social misfitness of being fat as a child. We are all social misfits. In some of our lives the misfitness shows, and in others it is unseen. But it is within each of us if we are honest. Why pretend? Why waste the energy to ward off the void that is waiting to be revealed and that can lead us to the central mystery of each of our lives—the mystery that will never be answered or filled this side of the Beatific Vision?

I am not saying that "Misfits, Unite!" is the answer. Would that all misfits were united, since all of us are misfits, not belonging to this world alone. Were all misfits united, then self-giving, sacrifice, compassion, stretching to understand the other, not running from the void, and the open communication of Trinitarian life intended for all of us, would be ours.[2]

But we do run. The running away from the gateway to the void is most clearly felt in our trying to fit in to the cultural and social norms set up by others. In doing this we are not only negating our histories, painful as they may be, but we are also negating the waiting God Who doesn't laugh. We are running from the God Whose Son didn't fit this world but didn't run from it. Jesus acknowledged His misfitness and, through all the accompanying feelings and realities of it, walked into the waiting love of the Trinity Whose expression His self-emptying love revealed.

Scars Transformed into Spirit More Solid than Stone

In His walking, Jesus felt peace—not the world's peace, but rather a peace not of this world. In other words, once social misfitness is embraced, the world's definitions of what it means to succeed, fit in—indeed, what it means to be a human being—are seen as hollow. Once these dimensions are seen as hollow, so is peace as the world defines it.

The peace of Jesus is not worldly peace, the warm, secure, safe feelings so often associated with peace. The peace of Jesus is that which comes with knowing in faith that I am right with the void. I am not betraying that inner hunger that beckons me to stand at the gateway and remain open to mystery. In embracing my social misfitness and turning away from all that calls me to fit in to this world's definitions of personhood, I live with a felt spiritual hunger that evokes the void. I live with an awareness in faith that becomes my anchor, my guide, and my shunt to the divine life manifested in creation through the self-emptying love that Jesus lived.

Our shunt, our anchor, and our guide to God is the felt social misfitness of ourselves and others. Felt social misfitness is, perhaps, the least contrived entrée into the void, into what faith tells us awaits, the God Who welcomes us through the stretch toward others, toward The Other. Felt social misfitness draws us away from fake goals that offer a pseudo-security that we are right with the world: "peace," security, being anxiety-free, friction-free, and feeling one with everything. To buy into all these fake goals is to take on the burden of striving for them by measuring up to the standards defined by this world: knowing when I succeed or fail and doing everything possible to succeed; knowing when I do and don't fit in and changing myself so that I do; arriving at success and still feeling hollow but pretending that I don't.

There is something, though, that unmasks the pretense involved in trying to measure up to the socio-cultural and even spiritual definitions of what it means to fit in. That something is the undeniable truth and memory of our felt social misfitness as children. Acknowledged—rather than buried—misfitness can bring us to the threshold of The Other.

We humans measure and are measured. The standards of measurement provoke derision and laughter at anyone and anything that doesn't fit. Psychology cannot take away the measurements or the measurers. Superficial psychology and what often is understood as spirituality can attempt to smooth over the rough edges of misfitness. But nothing can take away the scars left by the years of feeling that we don't belong. We don't belong. The scars of social misfitness can be the doorways and the sacraments leading us and reminding us that our spirits can never fit this world alone.

Yegudkin's transformation through suffering gave him the gift to play the French horn in a manner that was more solid than stone. He set Jack free. A paradox. The paradox is the fact that we try to fit in a world that can never contain us. The paradox is Jesus' self-emptying love in a world that grasps. The paradox is that suffering opens us to the God Who let Jesus walk into death as the only means of radical openness to the self-giving Godhead. The paradox is spirit more solid than stone.

"... I also remember all the *wondering* I did ..."

The sadness is that we forget what we knew as children. The wonder of childhood, more true than knowledge in that it opens us to paradoxes, is forsaken once we enter chronological adulthood. The roofless universe of authentic adulthood radically opens us to wonder. Indeed, an increased capacity to wonder is the hallmark of maturity.[3]

The following interview with Dorothy Day supports this truth:

> Dorothy Day resisted the attempts others made to see her life as something quite special—a preparation for sainthood ... I once asked her if she thought others had experienced some of the childhood spiritual experiences she described—had, like her, found their spirituality in childhood, as in the message that Wordsworth gives us in the "Ode on Intimations of Immortality": "Those first affections ... Are yet the fountain-light of all our day." Here is

what she said to me on the afternoon of April 20, 1971, as she sipped tea and thought about a life then drawing to its close: "In many ways I feel I'm the same person now that I was when I was a girl of nine, maybe, or ten, or eleven. You look surprised! I thought you folks [psychiatrists] believe we're 'made,' once and for all, in childhood, so why the shock?" She paused only because I insisted I wasn't "surprised," only "interested." (She clearly didn't believe me.) "Jesus kept on telling us we should try to be like children—be more open to life, curious about it, trusting of it; and be less cynical and skeptical and full of ourselves, as we so often are when we get older. I'm not romanticizing childhood, no. [I had mentioned that often we do.] I can recall my 'bad behavior' when I was ten (that's what my parents called it), when I got stubborn or sullen or difficult to deal with. But I also remember all the *wondering* I did, all the questions I had about life and God and the purpose of things, and even now, when I'm praying, or trying to keep my spiritual side going, and before I know it, I'm a little girl. Some of the things I asked then—asked my parents, my friends, and a lot of the time myself—I'm still asking myself now, forty or fifty or sixty years later!"[4]

The prelude to my escaping to China in 1988 was the intrusion of death into our family. My father's death and my sister's cancer, coming back-to-back as they had, my being on the "outs" with a segment of Maryknoll, and my no longer knowing for sure where I belonged were all received by the characters in "Redemption," seventy-nine-year-old George in what would be his last year in China, Xie Lau Shi, Eddie's "Where is Green?", and Norie's "White Yulan." All the facets of their misfitness called me back to the rear, right-hand side of St. Mary's. Who better than these misfits, poised between their "befores and afters," sensing from their unique vantage points the hunger to remain faithful to the void, to call me back?

I, who as a child of eight or nine decided I wanted a job that would allow me to tell others about the God Who doesn't laugh at us, was reminded by the most fitting people of the truth that had inspired my childhood and led me to my vocation. They mirrored my truth to me and gave me back my spirit.

When asked how spiritual concerns emerge in a person's consciousness, Dorothy Day responded in a way that reveals the pure truth of children's perception and how such ways of seeing remain with us:

> "No, I don't think spiritual questions have to be asked in a religious language. No, I don't think my own 'pilgrimage' began when I converted to the Catholic Church. I think my 'pilgrimage' began when I was a child, when I was seven or eight. You ask why then—well, I have a memory and to me it's the start of my life, my spiritual journey. I'm sitting with my mother, and she's telling me about some trouble in the world, about children like me who don't have enough food—they're dying. I'm eating a doughnut, I think. I ask my mother why other children don't have doughnuts and I do. She says it's the way the world is, something like that. I don't remember her words, but I can still see her face; it's the face of someone who is sad, and resigned, and perhaps she was embarrassed for the sake of all of us human beings, that we keep letting such terrible injustices remain...Anyway, I remember her face—she was troubled...Most of all, I remember trying to understand what it meant—me eating a doughnut and lots of children with no food at all. Finally I must have decided to solve the world's problem of hunger on my own, because I asked my mother if she'd take my doughnut and send it to some child whose stomach was empty. I don't remember my words, I just remember holding the doughnut up and hoping she'd take it and give it to someone, some child. I also remember her saying no, she couldn't do that, because the children she'd been telling me about didn't live nearby. I didn't eat that doughnut! I put it down on the kitchen table and I can still see my mother's face: she didn't know what to say or do! She was puzzled, and so was I!..."

"I...remember...being a little older, maybe ten or eleven, and walking with my father past some beggars on the street, and asking him if we could go and buy something for them—some doughnuts! He said no, we were in a hurry. I can see us right now in my mind, so clear! And I can feel my sadness and my disappointment. I remember, after that, walking by myself and wondering about the world, wondering why some people had so much and some people had so little, and wondering what *God* thought about such matters...It was then that I'd ask Him myself in those prayers I'd say sometimes when I was in bed and wide awake. I'd ask Him to tell us, to show us, what He thought, so we could do what He wanted us to do. Of course, I didn't know...that God had already come here and told us what He thought and how we should live and what the right things were for us to do!...I was a child with spiritual worries or concerns—and don't we all have them, I hope, and they start earlier than we think."[5]

To read Day's words, so direct and simple, about childhood questions and spiritual concerns is to remember how each of us in our own childhoods also questioned what would be and what we could do and what life and God meant. By simply *remembering* acts and feelings from childhood—things like walking past beggars and feeling sad—we remain alive spiritually. When we read about Day's sacramental doughnut, we "read" the sacraments in each of our own pasts, we recall the wonder and the spiritual questions that, all too soon, we buried or forgot—thinking that they did not belong in the world of adulthood.

The "journey which most of us fear yet desire, shun yet demand" is remembered anew when the artists in our lives such as Dorothy Day, Xie Lau Shi, George, Gardner, Eddie, and Norie appear. Through them the keen desire of childhood aspirations is once again awakened. We are reminded that we are yet guided by "the fountain-light of all our day, the master-light of all our seeing." Nothing can destroy our childhood wonders. How and when they are once again incorporated into our roofless universe of adulthood is a mystery.

Adaptation in the Lens of the Eye to Permit
Focus of Images of Objects at Different Distances

Person after person who received me in China reminded me that I had lost sight of my childhood wonder. I was entrapped in the disorder that had entered my life with my father's death, my sister's cancer, and my feeling cast aside by Maryknoll. I was paralyzed, feeling caught in a whirlwind over which I had no control. And the misfits in China called me home to the rear, right-hand side of St. Mary's.

They were all poised at the point between their "befores and afters," as I was. Xie Lau Shi was trying to break out of the confinement of the Cultural Revolution. Eddie and Norie were trying to live life without their parents. And seventy-nine-year-old George was relishing every moment of what he accurately perceived to be his last year in the mission of the China he so dearly loved.

I was poised between the before and after of my father's death and the disillusionment of realizing that, to me, "belonging" had meant belonging to standards of this world. I didn't realize it at the time, but I was fighting my father's absence and feeling cast aside by life as I had known it. I was running from the familiar reminders of him and life as I had known it. I ran into a barricade of misfits in China. They stopped my running and their barricade broke my limited vision that was confined only to the present.

Having made the geographical journey, I began the interior journey. Being in China enhanced everything I was seeing. I saw that social misfitness and its isolating connection are universals in life—not particular to any culture or age. Chinese and American misfits, though arriving at acknowledgement of their situations by different means, feel the same disconnection from their culture *and* the same hope.

Eddie's "green" was my rear, right-hand side pew in St. Mary's. In his poem he wrote that he was still waiting for the peace of green. His waiting recalled mine. His hope is mine. Norie's white magnolia, pure and holy, is left *in bloom* as her comfort and her reminder. I have Xie Lau Shi's gardenia and the students' white paper flowers.

Before going to China, I had felt only the scars of my life, and I was trying to hide them—to run from them. They went with me to China and leapt with joy and in recognition when they encountered Xie Lau Shi, George, Eddie, Norie, Yegudkin, and Jack Hawthorne. Acknowledging the disorder in our lives allows us to recognize the scars unique to each of us. Embracing the scars allows them to be transformed, with time, into sacraments.

In 1987, a few months before the intrusion of death erupted in our family, I had read a film review that said: "...the only thing worse than disorder in the universe is not to recognize it—which is, after all, the first step toward understanding and, possibly, accommodation."[6] I checked the dictionary because I wanted to have as clear an understanding as possible of the word *accommodation.* This is what I found:

> *accommodate* 1. To do a favor or service for; oblige. 2. To provide for; supply with. 3. To contain comfortably; have space for. 4. To make suitable; adjust: *accommodate himself well to new surroundings.* 5. To settle; reconcile...To become adjusted, as the eye to focusing on objects at a distance.

> *accommodation* 4. Reconciliation or settlement of opposing views; compromise. 5. *Physiol.* Adaptation or adjustment in an organism, organ, or part, as in the lens of the eye to permit retinal focus of images of objects at different distances...[7]

During those first two months in China, I was adjusting the lens of the eye of my soul. The artists of life I met were trying to reconcile opposing views of what they thought life was and what it was being transformed into through disorder. I knew, too, that they were trusting me with their attempts at accommodation.

When I was assigned the American literature course, George told me to "take it." He told me he would be threatened by my attending his Thursday night American culture talk. Eddie and Norie trusted me with their poems, their poignant recollections of the disorder in their lives and the adjustments they were making. Xie Lau Shi told me with piercing clarity that she had been different before the Cultural Revolution. I was recognizing the ever-deepening disorder in all of our lives. I understood that we were all making accommodations, creating a space that would bring us back to the interior void within which awaits the God Who doesn't laugh at us.

All human beings are subject to disorder. Foreign missioners' lives are defined by geographical and cultural disorder. There is something in our being attracted to this vocation that acknowledges disorder and wants to accommodate it. I firmly believe this. My belief is based not solely on my own experience but also on my work with missioners, both lay men and women and religious at various stages of their vocation—seminarians, women religious novices, seasoned male and female missioners—who have served in all parts of the earth.

Somehow those attracted to the vocation of foreign mission feel that their attempts at accommodating the disorder are best lived through straddling two cultures (host and home). The reconciliation, adaptation, and adjustment involved in their two-levelled (human and vocational) accommodation bespeak the unique and intimate connection between the vocation to foreign mission and what it means to be genuinely human. The foreign missioners' two-levelled straddling is the intensified journey of the saint and the artist of which Tracy speaks. The accommodation that the missioner's lens of the soul focuses upon is the seemingly distant approach of God, The Other, the Spirit more solid than stone. And the social, cultural, and geographical misfitness of foreign missioners is the unique lens that intensifies their journey and qualifies them as valid ambassadors toward the divine through the human.

Xie Lau Shi, George, Gardner and his characters, Eddie, and Norie were my missioners. They travelled into the void and beckoned me to re-embrace mine—to enter into that territory—at once so frightening and so intimate and familiar.

All of us want to fit. All of us want to be true to ourselves. So often these two desires are at loggerheads. Choices must be made. Accommodations are called forth. The desire to fit in is fundamental to the human condition. The fear of not fitting does not make us less human. It hearkens to the transcendent dimension in all of us that cannot be contained by this world. In straddling two cultures, foreign missioners stretch to accommodate the transcendent dimension. They speak to all humanity which is on the same journey, perhaps in a more hidden way.

Through what happened to me during my first two months in China, I knew I was with people who had entrusted me with their straddling. Each of them had been brought back to their interior voids in different ways. I remembered my "green" of St. Mary's. I sensed that this remembrance would reveal more of the sanctity to which we are all called. The winds were gathering.

4

"AND AS I LISTEN, NOW I SEE"

Green in the Green

Warbling the million silver trills
That with her mood may go,
In trees abloom on scented hills
She moves now high now low.

And as I listen, now I see
That locked in cage of gold
Never as in the woodlands free
So sweet a tale she told.

—Ouyang Xiu (1007-1072)[1]

"Beasts!" That was the first word I heard after listening to the Voice of America news report on Sunday morning, June 4, 1989, at 7:00 A.M.

I had woken up that morning after having listened with George to the radio reports until about 2:00 A.M. We knew that something horrible was about to happen. As soon as I woke up I turned on the radio and heard that the People's Liberation Army had opened fire on the students and citizens gathered at and around Tiananmen Square. Just as I heard the report, there was a loud knock on my apartment door. I opened it, and there stood Professor Guo, a professor in his mid-fifties with whom I had be-

74

come good friends over the past year. He exclaimed with hatred and disgust, "Beasts!" I said nothing.

We both stood facing each other—he in the doorway, and I in the apartment. I felt as if there were a miles-thick wall separating us, yet I wanted to be inside his skin. In silence he came into the apartment. I went into the kitchen, brewed him a cup of tea, and prepared coffee for myself. The two of us sat by the radio. Suddenly the transmission was filled with static. I frantically twisted the dial, trying to hear the latest details. The Chinese government had been blocking the V.O.A. in recent days. Old Guo said calmly, "Wait a while. It will become clear again." I wanted to say something to him, but I was too stunned, too angry. I was angry at the army and at all of us who had hoped against hope that this would not happen.

"If a mouse asked a cat not to eat it, would the cat obey?"

How could anyone other than a person with thousands of years of Chinese history flowing through his or her veins feel the true horror and defeat of the June 4th massacre? History wasn't changing. But we all thought it might have been possible that spring of 1989.

Waves of hesitation, elation, anger, hope, and forewarning had alternated, heaved, and blended over the preceding months in Wuhan and throughout China's centers of education and commerce. The streets in Wuhan leading to the bridge that links north, south, east, and west rail traffic across the Yangtze River had been filled wall-to-wall with students coming from the many universities in the area. Bus drivers had squeezed the students on to their already crowded buses. Truck drivers carrying vegetables to market from the outlying farmlands had also willingly transported students. The demonstrations had been calm and orderly. At the bridge, the students' banners, proudly bearing the names of their universities, flowed gently and high in the wind.

I went to the local intersection just once during those weeks. Two students, both Party members, had urged me to go. When I got there and saw the masses of orderly students walking proudly and with such spirit, I telephoned George from the nearest public telephone. I wanted him to see this. He had often spoken of the suddenness with which he had had to leave China in pre-Liberation days. He was thrilled to see what was happening; we were both very proud of the students.

George and I had agreed not to join in any demonstrations. We could always leave the country should something happen, and we felt that to join in and then leave would have been a betrayal of the students.

In the beginning and at the mid-point of the democracy movement that spring, it had been difficult to predict what would happen. George and I had opened our apartments each night to the students who marched in shifts—some getting sleep while others participated in the demonstrations at the Iron and Steel Factory, at the bridge, and at other campuses. We would prepare tea, coffee, cookies, cold drinks, and other snacks for them. The new shift would hear the reports from those who had returned. Returning students would get refreshed before going to their dorms where they'd shower, get some sleep, and then take their turn after the new group had come back. This went on for several weeks up until June 3rd.

We could hear strains of "The Internationale" almost every night. The air was charged with sober excitement, apprehension, and purpose during those weeks. Throughout the month of May, allegiances wavered between those wanting the government to maintain control and those supporting the democracy movement. Hope and fear, ideals and memories of defeat, and promise and threat chased each other those final weeks. We all breathed in and experienced the mixed feelings.

As the days and weeks went by, we would check the *China Daily*, the Party's English-language newspaper, to see whose photograph appeared on the front page. Whoever appeared on the front page—whether pictured on the upper, right-hand side or shown standing to the right of a power-person—was a wordless but telling indicator as to which "side" had gained favor in the past twenty-four hours. Of course, everything could have changed by the time the newspaper appeared on the stands. Everyone in the country, and in the world, knew that upper-level leadership was unstable; had it not been, the student movement would never have lasted as long as it did.

In mid-May I found myself talking with one of the seniors, who, to my knowledge, was the only Party member in our department who was not participating in the demonstrations. I asked him if he thought the movement would end in violence and, if it did not end in violence, whether those who had demonstrated would be marked for life by having information recorded on their personal files (which they never see, but are held by their unit leader who is a Party member). His response was sincere and without sarcasm, "If a mouse asked a cat not to eat it, would the cat obey?" If there had been even a hint of malice in either his voice or manner of expression, I think I would have asked him to leave the apartment—a rudeness almost unthinkable according to Chinese etiquette. But there wasn't; he was almost pained in expressing his opinion.

I could view and feel the Tiananmen massacre only through the lens of a Westerner with my sense of the dignity of the human person. I had read several books on what had happened to families during the Cultural Revolution. The horrors recounted in the books were confirmed by the many stories I heard during my first year in China: families separated for years, scholars forced into re-education on working farms, individual creativity and knowledge buried. And now this repeat of history for the sake of maintaining stability.

Yet the prevailing spirit of the Chinese would emerge once again. Coming as it did on the heels of my hoped-for escape from the roofless universe, my experience during this tumultuous time propelled me into a deeper awareness of the human mystery. These people, seen as individuals whom I had come to love and feel support from, carved into my soul an indelible admiration and respect for their spirit more solid than stone.

What happened on June 4th was radically at odds with everything that had preceded it. I am not referring primarily to the public student democracy movement. I am referring to what I had experienced during my first two semesters at the university. Coming to know the students, professors, and other people on a daily basis, talking with them and hearing their opinions, reading student assignments, discovering their kindness—all revealed to me what is demanded and can come through and from the human spirit. The genuine goodness and hope I had encountered all through the year made the June 4th massacre all the more evil.

Doubts about Whether or Not to Trust the Human Mystery

The students' responses in class had revealed a fundamental hunger for all things human. They had called forth from me a deeper appreciation and willingness to live life and to accommodate its disorder. The disorder evoked by their demands for more humane treatment from the government called forth an accommodation, a reconciliation, with all the qualities that distinguish the human.

Up to that point I had been moving toward reconciliation with myself and life through interaction with the students. Their demands upon me both inside and outside the classroom had made me willing to adapt to life with the disorder that had originally brought me to China. The day-in/day-out give and take between them and me was enveloped in my desire to thank them for what they had given back to me. On some level they must have been aware that they had brought me back to something quite fundamental, because I sensed it in their presence to the material we were handling in class.

As I look back on those months preceding the democracy movement, I see that from the time the sophomores wrote their poems in early October of 1988, I became more demanding of the students. I knew they had something to express and that they wanted the opportunity to express it. In the literature and writing classes I had asked them to dig into themselves and make connections with the material. I sensed and witnessed a willingness in them. I was digging into myself, too, as I prepared classes. I was alongside them in their reflection with my own.

Through this simultaneous awareness, theirs and mine, I became more and more sensitive to the fact that our perspectives differed. Characters in the stories who made me angry or toward whom I felt no compassion were seen differently by the students. They were seen as people to be admired or pitied. In the case of

Jack Hawthorne's mother, for example, I wished she had let her children know her grief rather than crying in secret. The students thought she was the bravest and most self-sacrificing member of the family. I didn't argue the various points with them, but I did sense a growing apprehension on my part.

What was underlying my give and take—their give and take—was something more basic than mere cultural points of view toward various characters in a story or ways of expressing opinions on various matters. While certainly clothed in cultural influences, the underlying question was: what is involved in being human?

I knew that in discussing literature and assigning weekly topics for the writing class, my approach was based on an inherently Western point of view. I could express my views on what it means to be human only through a Western perspective. Yet, in my mind and heart I was apprehensive. I found myself apologizing for being a Westerner and for inviting their reflections. I felt I had no right to ask Chinese students to look at literature or self-expression in writing from a Western perspective.

This is not to say that the students didn't constantly recall and discuss certain proverbs from Chinese culture that aptly described a character or situation. They often did. They would also use traditional myths and literary sources in their compositions. Yet, because they were so caught up in trying to appreciate the Western concepts in the literature, I feared I could be fanning flames of frustration in them. On several occasions when I asked for their opinions of literary characters or urged them to express themselves in their compositions, they told me that they had rarely been asked to dig into their own thoughts and express them. This was all during the first semester of 1988—well prior to the flowering of the student democracy movement.

I wanted them to think for themselves and to reflect on their own life experiences. They certainly were in the habit of doing this, but they were not used to voicing their reflections—especially in a classroom. They soon learned that I was serious when I told them at the semester's start that their life experience would be the filter through which the literature would find meaning and through which their compositions would come to life.

My approach and intention in the classroom was to reflect upon and address the fundamental issue of what it means to live life as a human being in this unpredictable world. My question to myself was, "Am I asking something of these students that will confuse, distort, or upset the way they perceive the world?" As I mulled over this question again and again, I realized that the authors of these stories had confused, distorted, and upset my own previous way of perceiving the world. In a way, this realization seemed to validate the approach I had chosen as a teacher of literature. However, as a missioner who is entrusted to be sensitive to the traditions and life philosophy of the host culture, I felt a little uncomfortable.

In my heart of hearts, though, I believed in the approach through the human—not on an intellectual level, but through the lens of the misfit. The students, who had passed stringent tests to get into college and now had a rare vantage point for self-reflection, did not fit traditional Chinese society. I was also a misfit, not only in a cultural/geographical sense, but also because I found myself poised at the threshold of The Other through having been touched by the death of my father. Moreover, it was through this lens that the authors had written their literature. So it was through this lens that I both hesitantly and confidently taught that first semester.

To be truly human is not to fit. To be truly human is to accept differences with rigorous empathy and then to push further, deeply into the mystery of it all—to the fundamentally human. I was comforted, strengthened, and inspired by the question posed and the answer given by Julia Ching in her work, *Probing China's Soul*:

> Which is more important: to be human or to be Chinese? To many people, this will appear a rhetorical question. And the answer should be obvious even if we are to change "Chinese" (whether the designation be ethnic or ideological) to "American" or "Canadian," "German" or "Japanese," "communist" or "capitalist." It is folly indeed to think that being human is less important than being this or that kind of human being...
>
> Coming from those of Chinese origin, the question seems all the stranger, since many associate humanistic wisdom with the Chinese tradition. But the question is

actually burning in the hearts of millions of people in China...In China...the importance of being Chinese refers to a loyalty that the state commands, which is to take priority over all other loyalties. And the state also defines how this loyalty is to be exercised.

I am writing this book to answer this deceptively simple question. I want to put it in no uncertain terms that I consider it (and I trust most people are with me here) much more important to be human than to be anything else. To extend this to ideological categories, I also consider it much more important to be human than to be Christian or communist (or "revolutionary") or capitalist. In fact, I believe that ideologies like Marxism and capitalism, or Christianity and Confucianism, should be judged by their fruits: do they make us more human, or less?[2]

I read Ching's words in the summer of 1990 after my second year of teaching in Wuhan. Reading them filled my heart with the truth of all I had been trying to live by and with the people in Wuhan. These people had brought me back to my own humanity—Xie Lau Shi, Eddie, Norie, George through his love of the Chinese and his vocation, and Gardner through his having touched off my openness there. How could it be otherwise, then? To be human, not Chinese or American or an adherent of any particular ideology, is the key to the hearts of all of us. To be a misfit within that humanity is to have perspective, a lens, that offers keener insight into the shams and the excuses and the methodologies we use to dodge the real heart of the matter—our humanity.

Ching's words confirmed so much of what I had acted on through intuition and faith. My doubts as to whether or not I was serving my needs or the students' learning, as to whether or not I had a right to let the literature speak for itself, as to whether or not I was fanning the flames of frustration—these were all just doubts as to whether or not to trust the human mystery. And the answer to those doubts was clear in the students' writing and in the expressions on their faces. Their desire to reflect on their lives was already there; it needed only a puncture from "outside" to let it loose.

When I read Ching's book in 1990, I felt a retroactive sense of relief. Her question—"Which is more important, to be human or to be Chinese?"—was evoked by the Tiananmen tragedy. Her answer confirmed the fundamental importance of humanity in the aftermath of the Tiananmen horror.

I have found that the same type of question is often brought forth when people from two vastly different cultures relate personally in times ordinary and extraordinary. The day-to-dayness of lives lived together manifests the basic issues of life in a high-lighted manner. The hurts, joys, pains, surprises, cruelties, and kindnesses—though they may be clouded over, evoked, or responded to with shades of difference—are universal to the human mystery and are less taken-for-granted when those attempting to live honestly together are from different cultures.

Anxiety Generates Strength: What Humanity Demands of Us[3]

One of the students I had in class for two years chose to write her B.A. thesis in the field of psychology. I was asked to be her adviser. As we met over the months of her research and writing, I learned that she was the third daughter born into a family with no sons. She told me that, since she had grown up in a small village, she often heard the story of how her father had wept the day she was born because she was not a son.

It was sad beyond words to hear this from a woman who had been born into a culture that highly values sons to carry on the family name, a culture that equally values respect for parents, and to see the pain she had carried for more than twenty years. I was the first person she had told. Her guilt at being born female had been kept inside until she had told a foreigner, an obvious misfit in her culture. The anxiety, guilt, and pain she carried because she was born female deserved to be communicated and the weight lifted somewhat through that communication.

I was honored that she trusted me enough to express her pain. As a Westerner, I felt sadness for her and anger toward the culture that had caused her to feel such pain and guilt. I didn't bother to try and "unearth" her anger. To have done so, I thought, would have been rather cheap and superficial. How could I even presume that she felt any anger toward her father or her culture?

What I did know without any doubt was that she had carried this pain and the anxiety that came with it for more than twenty years. And she had had the courage and self-respect to tell another human being, another misfit. What I could do, and hopefully did, was to receive her pain with respect and on the horizon of my own misfitness. My own misfitness as a human being was raised to a higher level of openness, to a "more than cultural" definition by my having come to China. To be able to extend that gift, in return, to a Chinese person was a privilege.

This young woman felt an anxiety that had been caused and evoked by a value her culture has held for thousands of years. The pain she had felt all those years was a sign of her health. She didn't—perhaps consciously couldn't—accept the cultural directive that she was less than good or had less of a right to be alive just because of her gender. She looked as if she fit in beautifully to her society and its cultural tradition. She was liked and appreciated by her classmates. She was often sought out as one who could listen well and understand. No one could have imagined the pain she carried. Wasn't it that very pain that made her so accessible and compassionate to the hurts and hopes of others? She did not culturally "adapt"; she maintained her pain. She did not sell out her self-respect so as to pretend that everything was "fine." And she told a person who obviously did not fit the culture that had tried to deform her spiritually.

Her pain evoked my own. Her courage evoked mine. She was born female. I had grown up fat. Her culture had told her she was less than good. Mine had told me the same thing. The reasons and impact were quite different, yet the ostracism was the same. I could get thin; she would have much more difficulty changing her gender. Yet the childhood pain and the scars of feeling like a misfit would remain.

This young woman had chosen to remain truly human by keeping her pain alive in her heart. It was a pain created by a cultural value that she did not accept. Her silent rejection of that value was broken when she told me. Yet the pain remained and was ever before her because she had grown up in a small village and was unable to leave her home culture. Whether or not she could geographically move, however, is irrelevant. I did move geographically, and the scars came with me.

The demand made upon her and upon all people to be truly human is to embrace anxiety as *the* means to interior health and generativity toward *life*. For her to have repressed her pain and to live as if she did not deserve to live would have been the "culturally right" thing to do. But she didn't! She maintained her anxiety, communicated her pain to one who fitted neither his own culture nor hers, and both were enriched. She gave me permission to use her thesis, "The Necessity of Giving Birth to Self," in my work in the States. Her own pain gave her an understanding that is communicated with conviction, clarity, and strength. Her thesis has given hope and support to those who read it with the eyes to see.

Like an Animal Startled by Strange Noises

The horror and inhumanity of the Tiananmen massacre awakens people. Unfortunately, we often remain asleep to the less obvious cruelties of daily life that go unnoticed and unquestioned, accumulating over generations until they are assimilated and become cultural values. This is true of every culture.

The acts of cruelty I saw in Wuhan were seen by one who does not belong to that culture, so they were highlighted. They also stood out more clearly because they coexisted with acts of kindness. In Wuhan I was challenged to become more accepting of the two-fold reality, terrifying and liberating, of true adulthood.

Seeing Xie Lau Shi laughed at. Seeing children's ideas and opinions ignored simply because they were children. Seeing professors run rough-shod over students. I was disgusted by the disgraces allotted through these acts. I know the same cruelties exist in the States. Their blatant acceptance in China impressed me because I am an outsider and also because I felt the hunger that reveals them as cruel. The human heart twists the graces of Chinese culture as much as it twists the graces of American culture. To a cultural/geographical misfit, the twisting is more visible, as are the genuine, humane values that come from the respect for the human so highly valued in Chinese culture.

Cultural/geographical misfits see through their lenses in a magnified manner similar to that of those who have lost loved ones and are poised at the threshold between worlds. What happens when these lenses cannot be put aside, or when the reality they reveal cannot be denied? Must foreign missioners try to ignore, adapt to, reject, accept, pretend, try to change themselves or the Chinese, or slough off cruel acts as mere cultural differences? Do those who grieve over the deaths of loved ones betray their love by pretending it doesn't hurt, by believing that the hole will one day be filled, by saying that God is a liar or that their faith has let them down? What is to be done with the magnifying lens of foreign missioners and those who grieve the deaths of loved ones?

The lenses of these two groups of people are so similar that the "anxiety-buffers" usually so at-hand to both now mean nothing. The escapes and anesthetics that come in varied forms in the home culture of foreign missioners and in the familiar routine of those who have lost loved ones are not available to the foreign missioner and useless for those who grieve. What faces these people and how can they continue to live in ways that are life-giving?

The only means open to these two groups of people are radically similar. I recall the truth that the missionary vocation claims its unique identity because of the void that constitutes it. Leaving home, loved ones, thought patterns, language, climate, and familiar ways of relating socially set the stage for the missionary endeavor. It is human nature to want to fill a void once it appears. However, if foreign missioners try to fill the void created by what they must give up to be what they are, then the vocation is lost.

There are many ways to try to fill the void: language-learning (learning more idioms than the members of the host culture, who don't have the time to learn them!); attempting to right socio-political wrongs; gathering in converts and counting the number of baptisms; becoming obsessed with possessions or feeling pride in the absence of them. All of these activities are necessary realities in the course of a missionary vocation. However, if missioners' unconscious motivation is to fill the void, they are no longer missioners.

Living with the void is missionary spirituality. What allows missioners to live with the void is a more radical dependence upon the fidelity of God. Such dependence upon God does not take away the felt void. More radical dependence upon God's promise allows the void to be acknowledged, felt, and lived with. The void in and of itself becomes the most direct shunt to God Who calls and sends missioners in the first place.

With regard to the second group, those grieving the death of loved ones, I remember that I first began to break through into the truths surrounding the death of my father when one day it dawned on me (and it felt like the sun breaking over the horizon of darkness) that I had felt similarly lost before. The first time was when I was twenty-four years old. I had gone to Taiwan as a seminarian for two years in Maryknoll's Overseas Training Program which comes mid-way in our seminary formation. After the glow of "everything's new and everything Chinese is wonderful," which faded after about two months of language study, I knew enough to have an idea of what I didn't know. I was disheartened, discouraged, terrified, and at a loss regarding how to live and face each day.

I happened to remember this in the aftermath of my father's death, at a time well past the point at which I thought the mourning period should be over. By then our family had experienced all the "firsts" without my father: Thanksgiving, Christmas, New Year's Eve, birthday, Easter. I thought we were "done" mourning. Then one day as I was walking to the mailbox I smelled freshly mown lawn. I burst into tears and felt instantly drained. It was completely unexpected. I almost felt as if I could see my father sitting on the patio with a cigar and a gin and tonic watching me mow the backyard. I was devastated. Was there nothing that wouldn't remind me that my father was gone? Would there ever be a time when I wouldn't be unexpectedly torn?

I was lost in time and circumstances. And then I remembered that I had felt exactly the same when I first went to Taiwan. And I had felt the same when I came back to the States. And when I first went to Wuhan, and on and on. Suddenly, I felt a hint of inner strength.

In the years since my father's death I have at times forgotten him, and then something or someone or some smell reminds me that he is gone, and I feel the empty-stomach feeling again. I have worked to fill the void. I have argued with God. I have prayed to "feel better." I have tried to forget God. Yet nothing can betray my love for my father or alter the truth that he is dead. To try to avoid the void is to be less than human. Death is part of everyone's life.

The bridge between the life of those who mourn and that of foreign missioners is a natural one. Voids are part of both. Attempts to fill the void are also very tempting to both. Attempts are made by both, and both fail to fill the void. What does a more radical dependence upon God *do*? What comes of it and *when*?

As someone who has failed to fill both voids, I have found that seeming answers to these questions should be run from. No one can answer these questions. The only genuine response to the questions is to know, over time and with trusting intuition, that the questions are honest. Period. Because the questions are honest, they are faith—the "short blanket on a cold night," as C.S. Lewis defines it. I'm grateful for some warmth, and I wish I had more. I know the night is cold; I know the void.

Gradually, as a missioner lives with the people of the host culture, a love develops for the humanness that shines forth and with which he *is* familiar. It shines differently, but it definitely shines forth from the deepest part of their souls, the void that unites transculturally. And for those who grieve the death of a loved one, something or someone gradually becomes a link, a spark, a connecting factor that pierces the void and draws forth from the void a heretofore unnoticed part of themselves that can help them begin to carry on again with care. The lives of foreign missioners and those who grieve the loss of loved ones are profoundly in sync.

This truth was once again revealed to me in Wuhan. I felt raw again. I thought I was "done" with what I had learned from my father's death. How cold and functionalistic that sounds to me now. The humanity that shone forth from Xie Lau Shi, George, Eddie, Norie, and so many others shed its light into corners of my soul that had been dormant since I had sat in the rear, right-hand side pew of St. Mary's and so clearly known God's love and goodness. This is what it means to be truly human, and remembrance of it soothes, hurts, challenges, and sustains us toward eternity.

As time went on in Wuhan, I saw more and more starkly what humanity demands of people and how we respond in ways both terrifying and liberating. From the depths of my soul I remembered that God doesn't laugh. God "asks our pardon" that this

way is the only way to communicate the Godhead and to remind
us through others that we were not created to be laughed at. We
were created to stretch toward The Other through others.[4] Foreign
missioners and those who mourn are beacons of the stretch.

During my time in Wuhan I came to feel I was one among
many misfits. Questions regarding what constitutes humanity
came to the fore. Through the lens of the geographical/cultural
misfit I saw the interior misfitness of others in a way that was not
threatening. I was "green in the green." Poised as I was between
two cultures, I was reminded more and more of the void left by
my father's death, and I saw with more sight, heard with more listening. I was like an animal easily startled by strange noises. The
strange noises were the noises of the beauty of human potential.
As I asked the literature students to consider the life crises of each
of the characters and asked the writing students to dig into their
own observations of life around them, a deeper trust in their intuitions and mine was being brought forth. A deeper trust in humanity was taking place. I knew it even then.

Enjoying It All:
Tea and Cookies, Time, Inspiration and Laughter

Little acts took on great significance. My neighbor across the hall,
the one whose son I had awakened to open the door my first night
in Wuhan, was a woman in her early sixties. She had striking
hands. They looked like my Lebanese grandmother's hands:
strong, gnarled, smooth as leather from years of hard work. My
neighbor and I would meet on the stairway we shared outside our
apartments and we'd say, "Good morning" to each other. We
would say nothing more, although she had a bright smile that
changed her face into one big smile. I wanted to get to know her,
but I thought it might be wise to move slowly and not come
across too boldly.

There was an open court between our building and the six-
story residence across from us that housed retired cadres. It was
the senior citizen croquet court. They played every morning, afternoon, and evening, spending several hours each day practicing.
They took the games quite seriously and carefully maintained the

court, making sure it was always flat. Everyone on the team wore a uniform with a number. On occasion they would play senior citizen groups from other units, and sometimes fierce arguments would break out. Mrs. Liang, my neighbor, was captain of the croquet team.

One day when the croquet team was warming up for a match with another team, I took some photographs of them from my second-floor window. The photos came out quite well, and I showed them to Mrs. Liang. She was delighted with them and, in Chinese heavy with a northern accent, began to tell me more about herself. She explained that she lived with her son, his wife, and their one son. She had been the principal of the primary school for faculty and staff children and had lived in the apartment for more than twenty-five years. She asked if she could have the negatives of the photos, since she wanted to make copies. I told her I would take care of making the copies and had 5 x 7 prints made for each of the team members. I gave them to Mrs. Liang to hand out. Everyone was thrilled, and I was grateful to have come to know this woman.

Every Sunday morning I could hear a "chop, chop, chop, chop" sound, and I knew Mrs. Liang was making *jyaudz* for her family. These steamed dumplings are absolutely delicious, and since she was originally from the North, I guessed she'd make them especially well (northerners eat more noodle dishes than southerners). My guess was right, as I discovered when she brought me over a dish of *jyaudz* one Sunday evening. This became a ritual each week. She loved to watch me devour them!

One day Mrs. Liang arrived at my door looking pretty official. She was dressed in a special-looking sweater and was carrying a gift in her hands. She bowed and said she was representing the university's croquet team and wanted me to have this gift. I received her with a bow, invited her in, and accepted the gift with two hands. It was a pair of marble "healthy body balls" (a literal translation) in a beautiful box. I tried spinning the balls in the palm of one hand with some success. She got a kick out of that and laughed!

Mrs. Liang noticed everything in the apartment. One of the students had painted a rooster for me. He was from the same province as Mrs. Liang, so she wanted to tell him what a good job he had done. I took a photo of her sitting next to the painting. We had tea and ended this special visit. She began to look after me, and for the most part, I enjoyed it. I would show my gratitude by getting some candy once in a while for her grandson. I was feeling more brought into the relational rituals of these people, and I felt full in my heart.

I learned, little by little, about Mrs. Liang's history. Her husband was an intellectual who had been in the hospital with next to no care during the Cultural Revolution. People at the university risked punishment to take her to visit him. I learned who these people were. I saw how Mrs. Liang still treated them with respect and special acts of kindness. I cherished the way memory and friendship were so closely united. It reminded me of the Lebanese and Italian ghettos where I had grown up as a child. Mrs. Liang was a hearty woman who visited the sick, exchanged recipes (or, more accurately, tried to out-shout people explaining that hers was the correct way to prepare a dish), and filled me in on the local gossip.

From the time of our arrival, George and I would hear loud screaming in the middle of almost every night. It sounded almost like a madman's shriek or like someone waking up with a nightmare. I asked Mrs. Liang about it. She told me it was a deaf child whose parents had recently left for work in a special economic zone in southern China. The child was living with a distant relative, and he missed his parents terribly. Mrs. Liang explained that he was going to a special school nearby for deaf and blind children.

She pointed out the child to me one day. He was about ten and had bright eyes and an alert smile. I noticed that a few children would play with him once in a while. One in particular was very kind to him, and they both enjoyed each other's company. I began waving to the deaf child, and he would nod his head with conviction and smile. Every time I heard him screaming in the night, my heart would break. I wanted to get to know him, but again decided it best to move slowly.

One day Mrs. Liang introduced us. We shook hands. I asked her to write him a note inviting him to bring some friends and come visit someday. She gave him the note and showed him that I lived across the hall from her. He smiled, nodded, and gave me a "thumbs up" sign. The smile, nod, and "thumbs up" were his way of saying hello to me from then on. He was yet another misfit who mirrored to me all that social misfitness brings with it. I wanted to know how this bright young child thought about the void and how he lived with it. I would wait.

I felt that I had time. Everything was going along beautifully. The literature and writing classes were a challenge that I loved. Every time I prepared for them I felt enthused. The conversation class was just fun—two hours of hamming it up with the students, listening to their pronunciation and rhythm, and encouraging them to speak more and more. I was also getting to know the teachers. The young ones would come to visit. I knew who was interested in whom and who was dating whom. I made cup after cup of tea and would always flush the leaves down the toilet until I learned that tea leaves are good for certain plants. George and I also went on cookie shopping expeditions about once each week. (George had quite a sweet tooth, and so do I.) The students loved the hospitality. They started bringing sweets, pickled fruits, and other snacks they enjoyed.

Old Guo also started coming to visit and chat. He'd show up about once a week and we'd talk about everything—people on campus, their histories, the Cultural Revolution, Chinese art, and campus politics. Slices of life filled my days, and it felt wonderful.

It was at this time, in mid-November 1988, that the university's director of the Foreign Affairs Office asked me not to look into teaching at another school the following year. They wanted me to return to Wuhan University of Technology. I was thrilled! How different this was from the way I had felt when I received the first invitation from them in the mail just a few months ago. Everything in my life had been awakened through reading Gardner's "Redemption." Indeed, I was set free to enter into life again.

The news of my being invited to return for the following academic year spread like wildfire throughout the university and even into the shops along the street where I'd buy cigarettes. I felt more at home than ever. Knowing I would return the following academic year threw a different light on everything. I began perceiving things more slowly, savoring the faces, the gestures, and the conversations with more ease and presence.

Strangers I'd never spoken with before would come up to me on campus and congratulate me for being invited to return. They

all knew I spoke Mandarin, so they didn't hesitate. Xie Lau Shi
was so pleased! I loved her visits to the apartment. She'd always
come with food. We'd sit and chat for a brief while. Mrs. Liang,
of course, was proud as a peacock that I had "done her proud." I
was beginning to see "the school-is-a-world-unto-itself" syn-
drome at play. It was exactly the same at Maryknoll and Duquesne and, I'm sure, at all schools.

The politics of the place were all-consuming, and I could already sense people wanting me to take sides or lean toward their
opinion in some way. I'm sure if I hadn't spoken the language I
would have been saved many a headache, but I would also have
missed out on hearing about their hopes and heartaches, their histories and defeats and joys. I found myself thinking of and praying in thanksgiving for the demanding language teachers I had
had in Taiwan more than twenty-five years before. They were a
perfect introduction to the culture of these wonderful people.

Encouraged Not to Crawl Back into the Roofed Universe

Knowing that I had another year with the juniors, I penetrated
more deeply in the literature course. We examined carefully the
crises in each of the main characters' lives. To facilitate the inves-
tigation, I traced the etymological development of the Chinese
written character for "crisis," a person standing alone atop a cliff.
One day in class, I climbed onto the desk/podium I used in the
front of the classroom. While standing there I asked the students
how they thought I felt up there. "Afraid, in danger, lonely, at risk,
unbalanced, embarrassed if someone outside the classroom should
look in, quiet, anxious, foolish," were their responses. I then
asked if they could think of any advantages to my being up on the
"cliff." They seemed puzzled for a while, and then one student
said, "You can see out the window better!"

I quickly elaborated on the response I was hoping for. "Yes! I
can see the campus greenhouse and the beautiful trees outside the
window that I couldn't see unless I was up here. I can see you differently from when I was on the ground with you. I do feel afraid
that I might fall off, but when my legs are steady, then I can take

advantage of being up here to see what the new perspective allows me to see."[5]

Together we easily made the application to how the characters in the stories could see more and differently through the crises they experienced in the disorder and unpredictability of life. We traced all the "befores and afters" and also the "durings" of each pivotal crisis. The written character for "crisis" in the Chinese language was a perfect entry into connecting the philosophical tradition of Chinese culture to modern-day literature. I suggested that the students use the wisdom of their heritage and its application to contemporary life to see what they could learn.

Without being inappropriately revelatory, several students said they could see the truth of the crisis-learning dynamic but only after the crisis had passed. I agreed, of course, and said that the durings of any crisis are the times when our legs are as yet unsteadied on the cliff. We all appreciated the truth of these students' observations. With classes coming along so well, learning what I was learning about trusting in the roofless universe and unlearning what I was unlearning about expectations of terror without a roof, I could almost see God's hand daily directing me.

I was also especially happy that the students as well as the teachers felt welcomed in my apartment. The university had neither time limits nor restrictions on visitors. I was going through tea leaves and cookies as if there were no tomorrow. Groups of six, seven or eight would come occasionally to wrap and cook *jyaudz*. It was comforting to know they felt at home in the apartment. Mrs. Liang would smile with approval also.

There was one group in particular with whom I felt particularly close. They were four senior women who were known as The Gang of Four. Their personalities were very different, yet they got on very well together. They came often to the apartment. I remember one telling me that her favorite film of all time was "Gone with the Window!" They could laugh at themselves and at me, and I had no problem laughing at myself or at others who knew me well enough to know I meant no harm.

Over time, these four seniors came to be known as my "Dry Little Sisters," and I was their "Dry Older Brother" (or "Uncle"— a sobering reminder of age!). In China, a "dry" relative is one who has no blood connection but is often closer in feeling than a blood relative.

My dry little sisters were fun to be with, inclusive, and kind to me and to others. I thoroughly enjoyed their company. When they were at the apartment, no one felt excluded from entering and joining in the visit. One of the Gang of Four was from the same province as Mrs. Liang, so she also felt a connection to them. Sometimes they would come and cook, and Mrs. Liang would often pop in and offer suggestions for the cooking. When the boyfriends of the Gang of Four visited them, they would bring them along to the apartment to visit. I was so proud! I did feel like their older brother (or uncle).

Something happened right before Thanksgiving that almost put a damper on everything. One of the younger teachers in our department who was in the habit of visiting with his wife came over alone one night. He told me that in the Foreign Language Department Party meeting that afternoon, my name had come up for discussion. It was mentioned, he told me, that students were coming to my apartment rather frequently and there were "questions" about me.

I listened with moderate interest. I asked him, a very sincere man who was not a rumor monger, what he thought of this. I asked if he thought I ought to be concerned. He skirted around the question. My mind was racing. I asked him if there was any inference that I might be "looking for a woman." He didn't say no. I was furious. I was hurt. I knew there couldn't be any question as to my professional teaching ability or sense of responsibility. So I figured if anyone wanted to drag me down, it would most likely be through suggesting that I was "putting the make on" the students.

I had a hunch who this teacher/Party member might be. She was a faculty member, one of the many vice-directors in our department, and she lived in a row of apartments right behind mine. I thought she was a smiling tiger; I distrusted her from the first welcome party we had. She reminded me of relatives in my family who, while attending a wedding and looking friendly and gracious, are trying to figure out if the bride is already pregnant. They smile at the bride and then turn and gossip under their breath with other relatives.

As I got up off my chair to get my coat, I told the young teacher that I wanted to visit Mrs. Dou right then so I could have this out and put a stop to any further rumors or misunderstandings. I was filled with rage, and when I am angry, my Chinese flows like a flood. The young teacher blanched, his eyes popped out of his head, and he jumped out of his chair and said, "No! This is China! You cannot do that!" I told him that if Mrs. Dou had any questions about me, she should come and discuss them with me. I knew this would never happen in China, but I wanted to say it anyway.

I asked the young teacher if there was anything he had been directed to tell me. He asked if I thought that was why he had come to visit me. I said that I did. He was both angry that I had guessed correctly and somewhat sad because, he said, he was afraid it might affect our friendship. I assured him it wouldn't. He finally offered the suggestion, coming from vice-director Dou, that perhaps I ought to invite the students less frequently to my apartment. I told him I had not invited, they had come on their own because they felt welcomed and knew I would not be rude to them. He said he thought I should follow the directive to get on the good side of Mrs. Dou. I refused. I also suggested that he tell Mrs. Dou that English language learning does not take place only in the classroom—and that learning about American culture also happens when the students visit. I finished by asking him to remind Mrs. Dou that the Foreign Affairs Office director had already invited me to return for the following academic year, so there was no question with regard to my professional ability or character.

I was livid. He knew it. And I knew that he would tell Mrs. Dou and probably the entire department membership, both Party members and non-Party members (who, I was certain, already knew about this entire matter) about my reaction.

The next day I told George what had happened. I needed his wisdom and perspective. I also knew that he had lived through being expelled from China in pre-Liberation days. He was furious. I loved that in George. He never pretended to have a perspective he didn't have. He was an honest man. His anger helped me to feel that I wasn't over-reacting. Neither of us knew why this was happening. He assured me that this was the way the Party

worked. They were suspicious of everything. He pointed out that I
knew my conscience was clear and added that this knowledge
would have to see me through. He said he'd keep his ears open. I
knew I could count on his judgment.

I also asked Old Guo about the matter. He assured me that
Mrs. Dou was not an evil woman; according to Old Guo, she was
just an envious person who was probably trying to make points
with someone for some reason.

I was bothered by this for about two or three weeks. I resent-
ed being watched, especially when I knew there was nothing to
watch. I was worried, not only for myself, but also for the students who came to visit. Would they be watched? Could this be
held against them if someone wanted to find something to hold
against them?

I mentioned it to the Gang of Four. They said Mrs. Dou was a
miserable person who always did such things. I knew the seniors
were concerned about job placements that would be coming up
the following spring as graduation approached for them. Mrs.
Dou, being a vice-director within the Party, could have some influence with regard to where these four might be placed. I encouraged my four dry little sisters to take this into consideration and
assured them that if they wanted to visit less frequently, I would
understand. They said, "Mrs. Dou can go to hell!"

Knowing that Mrs. Dou was in the habit of acting this way
and that it was more an expression of her personality than an exercise of authority eased the situation for me somewhat. The students said that I should try to flatter her—give her some face—as
false as it might be. "It's China, Larry. This is our way. We know
the games we are playing. That is all that matters." How could I
not listen to this wisdom distilled over thousands of years?

Offsetting the obstacles presented by those who seemed to fit
in China—basically those who belonged to the Party—were the
students and their work. I gave the sophomores another difficult
writing assignment. I asked them to write a composition about
their philosophy of life, to describe what principles guided their
lives.

I received the following composition from Flora. Reading it
dispelled whatever doubts had arisen in response to vice-director
Dou's tactics to curb my presence to and open respect for the stu-

dents. So often their work dispelled the doubts I battled with, doubts regarding my own temptation to conform and not question, doubts that wanted me to crawl back into a roofed universe. Flora's composition was a confirmation of everything I had felt in the rear, right-hand side pew of St. Mary's. My heart filled as I read it:

"Laughter, Tragedy"

Finishing my weekly writing, I went briskly downstairs from the fifth floor of the library. A burst of laughter following along with dance music in a lively rhythm poured into my ears.

When I arrived at the first floor, I thought to myself upon seeing what I saw, "It's here! How surprising—a dancing party!"

Everyone was standing aside and convulsed with laughter. There were two men dancing, if it could be called dancing. I recognized the strongman in a red, dirty sweater. He is an "idiot," a simple man, who lives nearby. He was jumping with his four limbs like a monkey, and the good-looking young man beside him was proudly directing the "red-sweatered." The audience couldn't help but laugh. "Look!" I thought. Some people were wiping their tears of laughter with the backs of their hands. Others were bending their backs laughing, and some were out of breath.

"A practical joke?" I thought. "Oh, no. It isn't simply that." I thought painfully, "This man is actually putting on a monkey show."

A modern-looking girl cried toward the good-looking young man directing, "I've never laughed so happily before! Great! Great for you!"

"Laugh once and you're ten years younger! That's it!" another beautiful girl said authoritatively. She seemed apparently satisfied with herself for finding a most proper phrase to describe the scene.

I concluded immediately to myself that according to her logic she is just like an ignorant, new-born baby.

Are these people more normal than the poor, ignorant man performing for them? What is beneath their
good-looking appearance? Who are the real performers
in this tragedy? I wonder.

Dumbfounded for quite a long while at the corner of
the library, I walked out leaving a look of disdain.

When I first met Flora, I saw her as someone whose presence
to other people seemed insightful and sensitive. She also struck
me as a person who was easily frightened, fragile like a fawn. I
wanted an opportunity to talk with her, to let her know she could
trust her intuitions. There were many students I wanted to affirm;
they seemed so hesitant to me. But they weren't.

Flora was a woman of strong character through her sensitivity. When I returned her composition, I asked her for a copy that I
could keep, and I also told her how I personally held a very similar philosophy of life. This composition created a feeling of understanding between us that lasted throughout the three years.

The students' untapped insights and their expressions of them
were flowing quite freely now, both inside and outside the classroom. So were mine. I hadn't felt this alive with an awareness of
the unroofed universe in a long, long while. I felt "green in their
green," and they knew it. They, in turn, felt green in my green.
The green was the sacred territory of the void.

One of the juniors, John, asked if he could come to visit. I
found this rather odd because most of the students never asked—
they just came. I said he was most welcome, and he wanted to set
up an appointment for a Wednesday afternoon. I was curious as to
what he wanted to talk about.

I soon discovered this young man was quite a deep thinker.
He thought about all the things the other students were expressing, but he took these things further: What does life mean? What
can be believed in? While taking pride in his heritage, he was also
questioning certain "virtues" such as patience. We talked about all
these things.

We ended up meeting almost every Wednesday afternoon. He
asked me early on if I was a priest or minister. I told him I was a
priest; he wasn't surprised. He had many questions about whether
or not there was a God. He asked me if I ever doubted. I told him

all the time. I assured him (and myself) that faith and doubt evoke each other. He was very curious about God, saying that he had been educated not to believe.

In the course of our Wednesday afternoon visits I expressed to him my ever-present concern that I always felt I should pray more. He quickly responded, "It seems to me that all your God cares about is whether or not you try to love, to be kind to people." How often I had found this to be true in the course of the years when this concern would plague me. Hearing it come from a man who was educated not to believe in God was for me a confirmation of the mystery of the Incarnation.

In the early mornings, before the university loudspeaker started blaring music, news, and the exercise regime throughout the campus at 6:10 A.M., I would get up, put water on for instant coffee, and then sit and pray the psalms and think about the previous day's classes and people who'd come to visit. The faces, ideas, conversations, and gestures of the students and teachers would come to my mind each day at that time. I would also get revved up for that day's classes. It was a silent, holy time for me each day. I knew God wanted me there in Wuhan. It wasn't just because things were coming together. It was a feeling that I belonged with these people who were different from me, but with whom I was strongly connected through the void in each of our lives, a void acknowledged and respected with grace and honesty.

The senior citizens were becoming more friendly and comfortable with me and I with them. I'd chat with them on my way to and from lunch and supper. I got to know their children and grandchildren. They also knew I would be returning for another year. The women would indirectly tell me gossip about Mrs. Liang, which I found both comic and sad. I would often hear the senior citizens talking outside my second-floor window. They'd relate to one another that I was the only son in my family. Their reaction to this seemed to depend on their mood; they thought it disgraceful, "How cold Americans are toward their parents—and not married yet!" or wonderful, "He loves China so much!"

In late November I became friends with a new group of people. I was returning to the university one day after a particularly "good find" on a cookie shopping expedition. As I walked up the back hill with two huge bags loaded to bursting, I overheard a group of young kids talking and laughing behind me. "Hah! Look at the old foreigner! He can't breathe carrying all that stuff up the hill!"

Since I had found such great cookies, I was in a good mood. So I turned around and said to them in Chinese, "Why don't you help the old foreign devil carry all this stuff?" They were stunned. Embarrassed, they immediately started praising my Chinese! Then they offered to help, and the four of them walked up the hill together with me. Of course they asked me what I'd bought, and I told them cookies. I also told them they were welcome to visit any time. They could tell that I was able to handle their joking about me.

The next week they came after school. They were middle school students, about twelve years old, and they joked with each other constantly. Because they had started learning "Englishee," we spoke the English of that day's lesson. They'd come about once a week and would sometimes bring their textbooks so that I could help them with a lesson. Most of the time we spoke Chinese, and I'd answer all sorts of questions about the States. They also started visiting "Old Georgie," as they called him. George would give them candy, and I'd give them cookies. They had few inhibitions compared with the adults on campus. They were neither children nor adults; I sensed their awkwardness as pre-teens.

There was one who was a real character. They wanted English names, so I named this one Joseph. He looked like my father in the photographs taken when my father was a child. I told Chinese Joseph why I had chosen that name, and he was pleased. Joseph was a natural; he had keen insights into people and situations.

One day when the four of them came, there were some young teachers from our department visiting. The spoken English of one of the teachers was rather poor. When I went into the kitchen to make some tea, Joseph followed me and said, "That guy's English is as bad as mine. He must have connections to have been hired as a university teacher!"

Joseph was poised at the threshold of adolescence. Several of the young teachers seemed to admire—perhaps almost envy—his street smarts. I knew Joseph would be facing and feeling misunderstanding rather soon.

Celebrations and Examinations:
Gatherings Exterior and Interior

The students asked me if I was feeling at all homesick. I told them that the only time I get homesick is at Thanksgiving, explaining that it is the time in the States when most families gather together. I also said that it is my favorite food holiday.

After having heard this, Flora and Norie arranged a dinner for me with most of the sophomores in their dormitory. They had obtained use of one of the administration offices (no small feat). They cooked a delicious chicken, apologizing because they couldn't find a turkey. It was wonderful! They had decorated the room and prepared several dishes. I was deeply touched by what Norie and Flora had done.

Before we knew it, Christmas was upon us. The students gave George and me beautiful cards, which I taped up along the doorways in the apartment. It was so good to read the notes the students had written. I still have them.

For Christmas Eve, the department had planned a masquerade dance. I went with a simple mask. George and I did quite a bit of dancing. He was quite the fox-trotter! I went home that night and celebrated Mass in the apartment at about 2:00 A.M. I knew God knew I was thankful for everything.

Very shortly after Christmas, the Foreign Affairs Office of the university began planning our travel for the three-week Spring Festival. During this holiday the university cleared out as everyone went home to be with their families. George and I planned to fly to Guang Zhou (Canton) to unwind for a few days before hitting the bustle of Hong Kong. We would take the hydroplane to Hong Kong and spend the three weeks at the Maryknoll House in Stanley. The Foreign Affairs Office director wanted our passports to buy the tickets for us. We felt uncomfortable giving him our passports, but he said that's the way it's done in China and explained that they'd be safe, so we gave them to him.

We heard nothing about final examinations for the semester, so George and I planned our own schedules. I'd have to read thirty final compositions from the sophomores' writing class and more than sixty essay exams from the junior and senior American literature classes. I scheduled oral exams for the conversation class.

I particularly enjoyed putting together the literature essay exam. The students were given a maximum of four hours to complete it. I was surprised at how many wrote for the full time. It was a cold, snowy day, and when everyone finished we went outside and took photographs and had snowball fights.

The exam I gave consisted of three questions, of which they were to choose two:

1.   Compare and contrast a life crisis in each of two characters' lives. Discuss in detail how each character affected your own life and what you learned from each regarding the meaning of love and death.

2.   Select two characters and discuss how each responded to the loss of innocence in his or her life. Please include how each was awakened to the meaning of life and discuss in detail your feelings about the choice each character made.

3.   In your opinion, which two authors most completely fulfilled William Faulkner's description of the duty and privilege of a writer? Please discuss why you've chosen each author and how he or she "uplifted your heart by reminding you of the courage and honor and hope and pride and compassion and pity and sacrifice" that characterize humanity.

The stories we had read and discussed that semester included: John Gardner's "Redemption," Bernard Malamud's "The Magic Barrel," Saul Bellow's "A Father-to-Be," Ann Copeland's "At Peace," F. Scott Fitzgerald's "Babylon Revisited," Irwin Shaw's "Act of Faith," Baine Kerr's "Rider," Joyce Carol Oates's "Gay," Langston Hughes's "One Friday Morning," and John Steinbeck's "Johnny Bear."

I was amazed at the students' essays. The time and effort they had put into reflecting upon these stories throughout the semester was evidenced in their work. Their ability to weave their own life experience into the essays indicated how the stories had evoked and supported their own feelings and insights into life. What was particularly gratifying to me was that in reading these essays I knew that the students did not feel alone in their perceptions of life. The authors had given name to the students' unspoken thoughts and feelings, and they acknowledged it with conviction.[6]

One senior, Robert, was especially helped by Gardner's Jack Hawthorne to remember and accept more fully his own father's death. In his essay he described how he had been in middle school at the time of his father's death. His mother hadn't wanted to upset his study, so he never knew of his father's death until he returned home for Spring Festival. As the eldest in his family, he was very close to his father, and he was heartbroken. From the way Robert expressed himself in his essay, I could see that Jack Hawthorne's life had helped him remember the pain and realize that he was not strange for feeling such pain. Robert described how Jack's feelings had helped him continue living in a way that could embrace the pain and, through the hole in his heart, be transformed into a more sensitive and alive person. Robert acknowledged and thanked Gardner in his essay.

I remember telling the students when discussing "Redemption" of how, when my father died and I was on sabbatical, I would cry almost every day. After several months of this, I became frightened. I went to see a psychiatrist. When I said this, the students had an immediate reaction. One said, "I thought only crazy people had to see psychiatrists." I assured him that I wasn't crazy and that I wanted to see a psychiatrist for help.

I went on to tell the students of how I had spoken to the psychiatrist for an hour. I had never met the man before. He listened very well and, after I had finished speaking, said, "Larry, I don't know you well, but you are certainly a man with many feelings and you are aware of them. Given the intense pain your family has been going through, if you weren't crying every day, then I would say something is wrong." I told the students how good I felt to be understood by another person and that oftentimes an author can offer people the same feeling of being understood.

While we were on the topic of "crazy" that day, I said to the students, "Who defines 'crazy'?" I asked them to consider people on campus who might be considered crazy. I mentioned Xie Lau

Shi. By that time, people knew that she and I were friends. I asked them to consider what might have happened in her life. I also asked them to be open to the possibility that someone right in the classroom that very day might be feeling a little crazy.

As I read through the juniors' and seniors' final essays, I could see that they had thought deeply about many things touched on in reading and discussing the literature that semester. What they previously may have perceived as "craziness" in themselves was broadened and deepened and absorbed into the fabric of being human and alive. Having read these essays, I found myself looking forward to next autumn when the sophomores would be taking American literature. Their compositions had revealed their readiness for the literature. They felt much more confident in the truth that their lives offered them food for thought and it was well worth expressing.

My birthday fell a few days before George and I were scheduled to leave for Spring Festival vacation. The senior men wanted to cook a dinner for me. Saying that they could cook better than The Gang of Four, they came to the apartment and spent the entire day chopping and cooking. George and Mrs. Liang came over too and we wrapped tons of *jyaudz.* The Gang of Four and several other women from the senior class joined us and we all had a wonderful time.

Early on in the meal, I realized that they were out to get me drunk! We all played the traditional drinking games. In my own haze of near-drunkenness I could see one of the senior men almost ready to heave his supper. The boyfriend of one of The Gang of Four, a fine gentleman from the Naval Academy, was present at dinner. He spotted the man about to lose it and swooped him out of the apartment just in time!

During the dinner I called Robert into the hallway. My father used to collect wheat pennies, and I kept them in his memory. I had brought a few with me to China. As we stood in the hallway I gave one to Robert in honor of our fathers' memories. He looked me in the eye and smiled. I knew our fathers were blessing our remembrance.

My four "dry little sisters" presented me with a beautiful medallion that had my animal year on it. It was a warm, joyous time. The men were proud of their cooking skills, and, by the end of the meal, all the food was gone—a good sign! George and I looked at each other a couple of times during the meal—glances that acknowledged the fullness and joy of this time.

After everyone had left I shut off all the lights, leaving one candle lit. I made myself a cup of coffee and went into the living room to sit and smile about the dinner. As I lowered myself into the chair, I heard a loud crash. I actually wondered where the noise had come from, and then I realized I was on the floor! I had completely missed the chair, landing full-force on my tailbone. They had succeeded more than I thought in getting me drunk!

The next day a few visitors stopped over to say goodbye before vacation. Madame Fei, the curriculum director who had offered the suggestion that I begin the literature course with the last story of the second volume, came and asked if I could teach a course on educational psychology. I thanked her, but said I had no background in that field. She explained that she wanted some interesting courses that would challenge the students with advanced language ability. I suggested family psychology, and her eyes lit up!

She also asked if I would teach a film course, using videos to help the students improve their listening ability and follow-up discussions of the content to improve their speaking. When I agreed to teach the course, she was excited and wanted to know if I could obtain materials in Hong Kong. I assured her I could. I asked her if these courses would be acceptable to the department leadership and if we could use the videotape machine. She said she would handle all that.

Madame Fei was a creative, professional and caring woman. She and I had many long and fruitful conversations during my three years in Wuhan. I had great respect for her appreciation of education and how it evokes, enriches, and supports a life lived more fully. As she left my apartment that day, I thanked her for the opportunity to teach these new courses. She reminded me that the writing and conversation courses would continue. I shook my head in disbelief that this was happening—family psychology and film!

Xie Lau Shi also came to say goodbye. She looked at me a little strangely and asked without hesitation if I was a minister or priest. I told her the truth. Then she said that her parents had been educated at a Protestant seminary. Her father had studied theology and her mother had played the piano and she had grown up at the seminary. She said all this freely and lovingly, and from that time on, every time we saw each other she would mention it. She asked if I could find her a book of psalms in Hong Kong, explaining that the Bible she had was quite old and the print was too small for her. I told her I'd be happy to get her the psalms. Our friendship was even more solidified.

When George and I got to Guang Zhou, we immediately hit a restaurant and each devoured three ham and egg sandwiches. I enjoyed being there with George. He appreciated a good meal, and we were starved for Western food. We bought lots of sweets at the many bakeries, ate pizza at the restaurants catering to Western business people, and sat and watched the television news and films coming from Hong Kong.

One day, George asked me if I had heard anything about his being invited to return for the following academic year. This was a subject that I knew would eventually come up, and I dreaded it. I told him with as much tenderness as possible that the deputy director of the Foreign Affairs Office, who loved George like a grandfather, had told me they couldn't invite him because of his age. Tears brimmed in my eyes.

The deputy director had added that if only George would be turning seventy-nine instead of eighty, they'd have been able to lie about his age. George looked at me and said, "This year was something extra—something I hadn't expected. I'm too old and they're embarrassed to tell me I can't be invited back. I know." I nodded, and he continued, "I'm lucky to have this year. I have one more semester... I'm happy for you. You're good for the students." He thanked me.

I knew it was an honor to be with George that year. So often I would see his face as he spoke with students. "He's looking on them with love," I would think. He knew his time in China was limited. He made the most of every single day, every party, every class, every time the students visited.

While we were on the hydroplane from Guang Zhou to Hong Kong, George told me about his first few years in China before he had been expelled. He and another Maryknoller had had to make their escape across a bridge when the Communists got to the teaching compound. As they had run across the bridge, it had been burning in flames behind them. George had kept in contact with several of his first students from the 1940s. Some had fled to the States, some to Hong Kong and Taiwan. When he returned to China in 1986, George went to the school where he'd first taught. The caretaker was still there and of course remembered George with great fondness. I knew George would try to find another school to take him when the next semester ended. His love drove him. I cherished our year together.

Hong Kong was marvelous! George and I and another Maryknoller, Tom Wilcox, a dear friend of George's and mine who had been teaching in southeast China, shopped, ate, and were treated like royalty by the Maryknollers in Hong Kong. The three of us embarked on shopping expeditions: Tom, knowing what he wanted, walked in the lead; George, stopping in every bakery, would pull up the rear; and I'd go into bookstores and video shops, emerging to find Tom standing up ahead, looking back and waiting. Then I'd look back and there would be George coming out of a bakery eating macaroons.

Tom and I went several times each week to select teaching supplies and gifts for the students: magazines, special books, scarves, barrettes for the women, ties and belts for the men. I got Xie Lau Shi a large-print edition of the psalms and George helped me select a beautiful dark pink wool scarf for Mrs. Liang. Maryknoll was generous in giving us budgets for teaching materials. I was able to find several good videos for the film course and reference texts for the family psychology course.

I went back to China with two new, full suitcases.

"It's not simple being a human being..."

By the time George and I got back to Wuhan, all the students had returned from holiday. They devoured the magazines which I placed on the coffee table in the apartment. Soccer, movies, home decorating, fashion, basketball—all were appreciated. Eddie gave me delicious tea leaves from his home province and several of the other students brought over special foods prepared by their families. It was wonderful to gather again.

The courses were set and got off to a good beginning. The juniors and seniors were fascinated by the family psychology course. In teaching this course, as in teaching the American literature course during the first semester, I was aware that I was approaching the material through the filter of the West. I was in no way suggesting that principles of Western psychology would necessarily apply to the Chinese family system. Nevertheless, while being sensitive to the differences between East and West, I also felt convinced that the truths I was attempting to cover in the family psychology course were universal.

My main thrust in the course was to illustrate the influences, both positive and negative, that are passed down in families, generation to generation. I hoped that the students would come to see and understand their parents as having been influenced by their grandparents, and so on. I also wanted to illustrate how we can change and how difficult it is to change, especially if we have been scarred at an early age and have not had the tools or understanding to stop the damage.

I stated my aims several times in various ways throughout the semester. I wanted the students to trust their insights enough to recognize that their parents weren't gods, but human beings with strengths and weaknesses like everyone else. To illustrate points I often used my family, especially the Italian side, since I think Italians and Chinese are similar in many fundamental ways: food, family, and guilt! Another hope I had for the psychology course was that these students would come to view their own childhoods in a more perceptive, compassionate, and understanding light.

The students had known me for a whole semester. They knew me well enough to know that I was approaching the material from a compassionate point of view, and that I certainly wasn't pushing any one way of understanding anyone or anything. In recalling the characters from the previous semester's literature and the way they had incorporated the material into their own lives, they knew that the enterprise of understanding people is complex and that change is painstaking.

The film course was interesting. I took things slowly, as I wasn't sure how the students could or would respond to the videos as course material and not just entertainment. I chose films that would capture their interest and have enough content so that I could teach from them. They loved "Fiddler on the Roof." I had seen this film in Taiwan and had been struck by the similarities between Jewish and Chinese culture with regard to family values. We also watched "Fame," "Zorba the Greek," "A Woman's Face," "Kramer vs. Kramer," "Dr. Zhivago," "Gone with the Wind," "The Sound of Music," "Top Hat," and "Singin' in the Rain." I'd introduce the story line, give a brief overview of the characters, and we'd watch about twenty minutes of the film. Then I'd stop the video and ask for questions. After viewing the film in twenty-minute segments, we would go back and watch the entire film all the way through with no stops. We did this for each film. Over the course of the semester, I knew that the students could handle the videos, and I began thinking about which videos I could use for the autumn 1989 semester.

The writing class was coming along well too. When it got a little dry, I would play music and ask the students to write about what they felt, or we'd watch part of a video and I'd ask them to write about it. I decided to meet the students individually to go over their particular difficulties with the writing. They were astounded that I'd do this, but I thought it would be beneficial.

Mrs. Liang was still bringing over the Sunday night *jyaudz*. She told me that she'd be moving in the summer to a new residence that was being built across the street. We both felt sad that we'd no longer be neighbors. She mentioned that her apartment was to be renovated this summer—as were each of the apartments in the building where we were living—and suggested that I move into her apartment once it was renovated. It had a larger balcony than mine and, since her apartment was in the middle of the building, it would be warmer than mine in the winter. I thought her suggestion was very kind and agreed that it was a good idea. Mrs. Liang had become part of my everyday life, and I would miss her after she moved. She assured me she'd still visit and bring me *jyaudz*.

The croquet games stopped for the winter months; it was rainy and very cold. One day I saw the deaf child on the court. We chatted through one of the other children who made gestures common to the two of them, their personalized sign language. I once again extended my invitation, telling him that he was welcome to visit my place.

It was at that time that I was viewing "Fiddler on the Roof" all the way through with the juniors and seniors. There is a point in the film when Tevye and all who live in their home village are forced to move; it's toward the end of the film. Tevye goes into the stable to bid his horse farewell. For years this horse has pulled the wagon that Tevye has used to deliver milk every morning. He cannot take his horse with him as they are fleeing the revolution. Tevye goes into the barn alone and affectionately pets his horse, saying quietly and with direct feeling, "Thanks for everything."

As I watched this scene, tears and the empty-stomach feeling came over me. I instinctively remembered my father on the night before he entered the hospital saying to me as I tucked him into bed, "Thanks for everything. I love you. You're a good boy." When Tevye said to his horse, "Thanks for everything," my father's face, voice, and smell came immediately back to me. Thank God the film ended soon after that. I got up to leave, and one of the students said, "What about rewinding the video?" I asked him to do it and to take it to my apartment as I had something to do.

I tried not to run back to the apartment because if I had people would have noticed and then come to see if anything was wrong. I got back and rested my face against the wall, crying and asking from my soul if I would ever get used to my father's death. I sobbed and asked my father for a sign that things would be all right—that I could take his love and continue in some way with the pain.

Right then I heard loud, incessant knocks on the door—very loud knocks that didn't stop. I waited, not wanting to open the door because my eyes were all sore from crying. The knocking continued, louder than I'd ever heard before. I thought someone must have noticed my almost-run back to the apartment and come to see if I was all right. When I went to the door, there was the deaf child smiling bright-eyed. He nodded and gave me the "thumbs up" sign, then motioned to enter the apartment. It was my father's response; I knew it! I wanted to hug the child, but knew I couldn't.

He came in and I gave him tea and cookies and sat down with him. I was so excited that I didn't even stop to wonder how the two of us would communicate. He got up and looked at everything in the apartment—noticing this and that and turning to smile and give me the "thumbs up" sign when he found something that interested him. He finally sat down and we both laughed when we realized we didn't know how to communicate. He started writing in Chinese. My written Chinese is quite limited, and there was no way I could read all he wrote or write back to him. I got out the dictionary and we both looked up words. I was so happy he had come to visit. He indicated that he wanted me to give him an English name. I thought of his bright eyes and chose "Lucas," thinking it might have its root in the Latin "lux" which means "light." I wrote it down for him in English and then wrote "bright, radiant" in Chinese to indicate what it meant. He smiled, nodded, and gave me another "thumbs up" sign.

Lucas started coming about once a week. He wasn't in the least intimidated when students or teachers were visiting. They, too, noticed how bright and gifted Lucas was. When others were visiting it was much easier for Lucas to communicate, as they could read his writing. Everyone remarked on the style of his written Chinese, saying that it reflected well on his personality and intelligence. (I'd often heard this in China, namely, that calligraphy reveals a person's intelligence and soul.) I was so pleased to see how the students related with Lucas and he with them. He felt at home with us. And my father opened the way for Lucas to start visiting.

I was feeling so good about Lucas's visits and the students' acceptance of him that I felt more confident in the family psychology course. I decided to get a little more specific with examples to illustrate certain things. At one point we were discussing traditional family roles assigned by society, such as, for example, the way parents are given authority and children, for the most part, are expected to obey their parents and take the lead from them. I told the students how, because I come from a traditional Lebanese-Italian background, the importance of respect for my elders had been hammered into my head.

Then I related what had happened at a meal in Hong Kong one evening. I had been invited by Chinese friends of a Maryknoller to join them for dinner in a restaurant. The family had two sons about twelve and ten years old, one quite chubby and the other with a stutter. In the course of the dinner (both grandmothers, parents, two Americans, and the two children present), the fa-

ther asked what I would be teaching the next semester. I told him I
was quite excited about the family psychology course.

The father then proceeded to ask me questions about his sons.
He prefaced his remarks by saying, "My sons won't mind that I
ask you this, because they're just children." He then expressed
concern about one son's stuttering and the other's weight problem.
He was apprehensive, fearing that his sons would not socialize
well or would be ostracized by their peers. I was appalled at the father's insensitivity. He was well educated and well intentioned, but
I felt very sad and embarrassed for his two sons. I told the students
that the father had certainly meant well, and they understood this.
Yet I also saw them wince when I described how the father had
said these things publicly, over dinner, and in front of his sons.

In relating this incident to the students that day in class, I also
mentioned that I had been a "fatty" and that my classmates had
laughed at me. I concluded the story about the Hong Kong dinner
by telling the students that I had responded to the father by saying
that these situations are common, that he shouldn't worry because
his sons would outgrow their situations if they weren't pressured
too much.

I then asked the two sons to show me where the men's room
was. Once we were away from the table, I did something that is
not usually done in this culture: I told the two sons that I was
sorry their father had brought up their situations in front of everyone. I then jokingly offered each of them a cigarette and suggested that they try not to be too upset by their weight or stutter. I also
told them that I had been a hugely fat child, but that I had changed
as I got older.

The students in the family psychology class felt the pain of
the two children. They also appreciated the father's concern, but
felt he ought to have asked me about it in private. Some of the
students said, "No big problem. Aren't you making too much of
it?" I agreed that it wasn't a big problem, but noted that things
like this—parents taking advantage of the position given them by
society, having no consideration for their children's feelings and
regularly subjecting them to embarrassment—could result in
greater, more serious abuse. Then I mentioned how in the next
class we would consider the emotional, physical, and sexual abuse
of children documented in the United States.

I based much of my presentation on the work of Alice Miller.[7] In her writings Miller details how the natural, spontaneous curiosity and wonder of children is often squelched by parents whose own parents did the same to them. Thus, the chain of abuse continues. Society supports not taking children seriously. Braving suffering, preferably in silence, is also praised in most cultures. Most cultures give parents the responsibility of educating children in the "banking style" (i.e., children are completely empty and must be filled). Most children in most cultures live to please the parents who are sources of needed affection, support, acknowledgement, and affirmation. Add to this the sense of filial loyalty prized by many traditional cultures along with "honor thy father and thy mother," and children are pretty much at the mercy of the family they are "thrown into" at birth.

In discussing the emotional, physical, and sexual abuse of children I mentioned often that I was using documented cases and statistics from the United States. I was acutely attuned, however, to student reactions as I presented the material. It was clear to me that the students were aware of the widespread incidence of emotional and physical abuse in China. At the time the *China Daily* was publishing articles on cases in which children committed suicide because of the pressure put upon them by parents to succeed and give them "face." I took the news articles to class as illustrations.

When I approached the topic of sexual abuse of children, however, student reaction was very different. They responded with revulsion and openly denied its occurrence in China. I had expected this.

I continued the discussion by explaining that the root cause of sexual abuse is not sexual in nature but rather revolves around a "powerful/powerless" pivot. For instance, when a person feels powerless for some reason—be it social, political, or psychological—that person will often feel the need to ventilate his or her feelings. Talking about the powerless feeling is the most helpful, least destructive, and best possible way to understand and deal with the feeling of powerlessness. However, in situations where talking with a trusted person is not possible or is discouraged, the person feeling powerless will oftentimes ventilate the feeling on something or someone who is less powerful.

As an example, I told the students what I had learned when I went to Guatemala in 1986 shortly after a very intense period of political turmoil to give a workshop to teachers from the United States. (It was actually a workshop on spirituality for Mary-knollers working in Guatemala, but I didn't go into this.) I described how several teachers had told me that many Guatemalan children had reported that they were either being beaten or sexually abused and that animals were also being tortured. The political pressure was so great and the feelings of powerlessness were so overwhelming that the rage was being taken out on children and animals.

I also used the example of highly structured hierarchical societies in which roles are clearly assigned and adhered to. Government, extended family, parents, and children all know their place. Children, who are assigned the role of obeying and pleasing their parents, are totally without power. They are easy targets for those above them who have no outlet for their own feelings of powerlessness.

Other information I presented on this topic included the fact that sexual abuse of children is not exclusive to class, social position, economic level, or educational opportunity. I presented data demonstrating that highly wealthy groups in the States as well as very poor populations both share in this most unfortunate phenomenon. I noted that the sexual abuse of children is a terrible thing and that no one wants to believe it happens. However, to pretend that it doesn't happen because we are shocked and disgusted by it only keeps us ignorant while children remain silent, helpless victims.

When the bell rang for the class break, one female senior walked past the desk/podium and, as she headed toward the corridor, whispered almost inaudibly to me without bending toward the podium "Say more." I felt relieved, sad, and grateful to her because I knew that if one student had the courage and self-respect to say this, then at least one-third of those present felt the same.

I did say more, giving examples of emotional, physical, and sexual abuse of children. I made clear and continually stressed the fact that the purpose of discussing the abuse of children was to encourage individuals to develop compassion toward themselves and to feel the pain that so often gets buried or is praised for being endured in silence. I knew that in China—with its hierarchical structure, its high regard for filial loyalty and the importance of saving face, and its history of political repression—sexual abuse must be rampant. I stressed in various ways the necessity of understanding these realities for the sake of breaking the chain of abuse and coming out from under the cultural deformation that blankets child abuse with silence. I was very clear in pointing out that every culture wants to turn its head and heart away from this truth. In the turning away is the continuation of victimization of future generations. I mentioned that the students themselves would be parents in a few years and that the best way they could be good parents was to develop and nurture compassion and understanding toward themselves.

During my three years in Wuhan, I always presented the same material on these three forms of child abuse. Students found it a relief to know that abuse could be talked about openly and with respect for the child. Several of the students came to my apartment and talked about their personal histories. When they talked about physical or emotional abuse, they usually came with a trusted friend. However, in discussing sexual abuse, they always came alone and spoke very hesitantly at first and then with open emotion. I was very thankful that they trusted me enough to talk about such a personal, delicate area. Their self-respect was evident in many, many ways. Discussing sexual abuse was one of the most evident.

The serious content of the family psychology course was not heavy in the sense of being overbearing. I felt a mature give-and-take with the students. The days were interspersed with dinners cooked at the apartment, card games, and a wonderful eightieth birthday party for George. It was a bittersweet occasion, because we all knew it was the reason why George could not be invited to return for the next academic year.

Joseph came to visit alone one afternoon. I thought it a little strange that his three friends were not with him. He sat down in a chair, placed his hands behind his head, stretched out his legs, and asked me, "How do you know when a friend is really a friend?" I asked if he was referring to a girlfriend, but he said, "No." He went on to explain that a member of the group, one of the school chums he'd always hang around with (Joseph did not mention his name), and whom he thought was his friend had said something quite hurtful about Joseph to another friend. Joseph said that he was surprised and that his "heart was hurt." He was very serious. He asked me again, "How do you know if someone is really your friend? How do you know if you can believe or trust someone?"

I looked at him and I realized that this twelve-year-old was crossing over into the complexities of life. I said, "Joseph, you are asking a question now that you will ask many times in your life. There is no guarantee or way to know for sure if someone is really your friend. You just have to pay attention, try and see." He sighed, looked at me again, and said, "It's not simple being a human being..."

"No," I answered, smiling, "but you have a very strong foundation to be able to ask this question when you are twelve." I was deeply touched that he had come alone and talked about this. We had tea and chatted about other things. When it was time to leave, he opened the door and, without turning back, he said in English, "Thank you." I can imagine how difficult it was for him to talk about the painful reality of being hurt by someone he'd thought was a friend. His ability to talk about it and his "thank you" were the best signs that Joseph would be all right with life's uncertainties.

The Whirlwind Begins:
Beatific and Demonic at Once

April 15, 1989, marked a turning point for everything that year, and, as things evolved, in modern Chinese history as well. Hu Yao Bang, a champion of liberalization and students' rights, died. Hu had been appointed Party General Secretary by Deng Xiao Ping and was subsequently scapegoated and removed from the position by Deng for not cracking down on the university students after their December 1986–January 1987 demonstrations. Hu was held in high esteem and respected by university students throughout China.

A sense of anticipation had been in the air since the New Year celebrations of 1989. Everyone knew it would be a year of commemorations: it was the seventieth anniversary of May 4, 1919 (May 4th Movement), the beginning of university students' participation in politics. It was also the fortieth anniversary of the founding of The People's Republic under the Communists. Everyone was talking about the celebration of these two events. Everyone knew there would be some expression of student unrest and demand for their rights on May 4th. Everyone also knew that with the failing economy at the time there would be some show of displeasure with the Party's performance. Hu Yao Bang's death triggered an early start to all that had been anticipated. Hu was seen as a man of integrity, sincerity, and selflessness. After having been scapegoated and removed from his position, he was held in even higher respect in the hearts of the students and all who felt a hunger for integrity.[8]

From the time of Hu's death on April 15th until the nationally televised memorial service on April 22nd, we all heard rumors passed along through a quickly organized and efficient university student network that relayed information from Beijing to all other universities throughout the country. No one believed the government-run televised news broadcasts or what was printed in official newspapers. Chinese people have been accustomed to reading between the lines for centuries, and footpath news is trusted more than anything else. I saw this happening and felt its movement as the weeks progressed.

According to Chinese law, gathering to mourn is permitted. The students in Beijing began gathering on April 16th to mourn Hu Yao Bang. The numbers mounted until the day of his memorial service, when those gathered totalled nearly 200,000 in Beijing.

Traditionally, in the history of student expression, the universities in China offering majors in history, political theory, and the humanities take the lead for all other universities. Since ours was a university of technology, our students were hesitant in their initial response to the events in Beijing. It would not be until early May that life on our campus was altered radically.

The students gathered in my apartment and George's to watch the televised memorial service to honor Hu Yao Bang. They wanted to see who would attend; they wanted to see if Hu would be revered by the Party. As it turned out, all the Party leadership gave tribute to Hu through their attendance. The students were pleased that the Party leadership had honored Hu's memory by attending the televised memorial service, but they also felt their attendance was a sham.

I could feel the genuine respect the students held for Hu Yao Bang. He had personified what happens to open-minded people of integrity who refuse to bow down to the Party's commands to maintain a facade and forsake conscience. A felt silence was in the air.

I do not remember clearly when television coverage of the Beijing demonstrations began. I know all the students and teachers listened intently, faithfully and daily to the B.B.C. and the V.O.A. All that people talked about throughout the month of April was what was happening in Beijing. We still had classes and students of course still came to the apartment. We watched the news avidly. The students would watch for any hints of what was behind the news coverage. We went on an outing to see the cherry blossoms and then rode around East Lake. But all we thought and talked about was what was happening and could happen.

As the May 1st Workers' National Holiday approached, the Foreign Affairs Office personnel asked George and me if we wanted to take part in a trip to Gui Lin that was being planned for the foreign teachers in our area. We managed to bow out gracefully. The trip would extend into May 4th, and we wanted to be at the university should anything happen on that day.

Rumors were spreading that there might be a major demonstration on May 4th. Students at Wuhan University and at the Normal University were beginning to organize all the local universities and colleges. George and I wanted the students to see our apartment lights on should anything erupt in our area. There was nothing we could do, but we wanted the students to know that we were home.

Student demonstrators in Beijing were joined by journalists for the commemoration of the May 4th movement. Students from Wuhan University and the Normal University came to our campus, demonstrating and singing "The Internationale." Our university began to enter the movement in full swing. Little bottles were being dropped out of dormitory windows. (Deng Xiao Ping's given name has the same sound as the words for "little bottle," and the gesture of breaking little bottles represented the hope that the government's policies would fall apart.)

Most students stopped coming to classes after May 4th. All the teachers were instructed to go to the classrooms every day and remain there for the two-hour duration of the class period. If one student came to class, we were to teach him or her. George and I went each day and waited until the education officer made the rounds to check each classroom. The demonstrations were given added momentum with the upcoming visit of Gorbachev to China—the first such visit in thirty years. It was scheduled for May 15th.

Every day, students from our university and from the entire Wuhan area were marching in orderly fashion to the bridge that connects north, south, east, and west rail and auto traffic across the Yangtze River. The streets were wall-to-wall with students carrying banners bearing their universities' names waving in the wind.

Vice-director Dou would go each morning to the school's gate to see which students from our department were demonstrating. However, when the news seemed to indicate that the winds had changed in favor of the democracy movement, she would remain in her home, appearing only when the status quo was receiving support in the news.

George and I were asked to direct the research and writing of some seniors' B.A. theses. I was given four students. They wrote on the themes of solitude, child-raising, and a comparison of Eastern and Western culture. One of my dry little sisters wrote on self-acceptance. They managed to do their research and writing even though they were spending hours demonstrating at the Wuhan Iron and Steel Factory, at other schools, and at the bridge. It was a whirlwind of activity.

Seniors were also scrambling to find jobs. If they didn't secure their own jobs, they would be assigned jobs back in their home provinces, usually middle school teaching, and they preferred to remain in the city where they had more benefits and opportunities. Finding their own jobs meant giving gifts to the right people at the right times. The students would gather in the apartment and discuss the art of "patting the horse's behind," as they called it.

In the midst of all this uncertainty, excitement, activity, and apprehension as to what would happen, George and I planned a graduation dinner for the seniors in the teachers' dining hall. We felt it was a meaningful way of showing our respect and wishing them well as they prepared to graduate. Working with the dining room staff, whom we came to know quite well, we planned the menu and arranged to hold the dinner from 4:30 to 7:00 P.M. on May 19th. The seniors were thrilled with it all. Several had their hair done in a special way, and they all dressed for the occasion, even though some came in all sweaty from their shift of demonstrating.

That night, May 19th, the Premier of China, Li Peng, declared martial law in parts of Beijing. His speech was televised and we could see that the auditorium where he made the announcement was filled with people in military dress. The students who were in my apartment watching the speech left immediately to plan their response. I know some marched to the Iron and Steel Factory that night.

The deputy director of the Foreign Affairs Office came to my apartment and said that he thought it best to begin the process of getting my round-trip ticket to the States and back to China as I would be returning in late August. He wanted my passport. I asked him if there would be any difficulty, what with martial law in place. The ticket had to be purchased in Beijing since it was an international flight and such tickets for our university were purchased through the Bureau of Building Materials in Beijing. I was assured there would be no problem with either the passport or with martial law.

I gave him my passport. George would be flying to Hong Kong, so his ticket could be purchased in Wuhan as was the case when we went there for Spring Festival holiday. The two of us were supposed to leave toward the end of June. George expressed some concern about my not having my passport. He said that there was no telling what might happen with the student demonstrations. I was concerned also.

It was during this time that George and I kept our apartments stocked with cold drinks, cookies, snacks, and tea to refresh the students as they returned from demonstrating, coming and going in shifts. It was also at this time that the senior who hadn't attended the demonstrations said to me, "If a mouse asked a cat not to eat it, would the cat obey?" The director of the Foreign Affairs Office came to each of our apartments and officially explained to us what was happening. George and I listened with respect. We were told not to encourage the students and also not to join in any demonstrating. Of course, George and I had already made this decision, since we had no idea what the outcome would be. We could not in conscience take advantage of being foreigners.

All of the teachers were still going to the classrooms every day even though it had been over two weeks since we had had any students from our department come to classes. A student delegation from our university had gone to Beijing to join students from many other schools throughout the country in the Tiananmen Square demonstrations. A banner with our school's name on it was seen amidst the sea of students on the televised national news broadcast. Everyone on campus was talking proudly about it.

I had an encounter with vice-director Dou during this time. I was in the classroom one day waiting to see if any students would show up. Vice-director Dou had a scheduled class at the same time and was waiting alone in the classroom across the corridor from mine. The education officer had already made his rounds, and, just as I was getting ready to return to the apartment, one junior who was taking the class I was scheduled to teach came down the hall. Vice-director Dou and I both saw him. He was a Party member. Dou got her smiling tiger face ready for him and said, "So you came to class! Only you are a good student!"

As the three of us were standing in the classroom corridor, the student said to me, "Will we have class?" He spoke in English. Dou could not speak English; she taught another foreign language. I repeated his question back to him in Chinese so that she would not think he and I were exchanging any other information, and then I said, "It's your decision. If you want to have class, I will teach." He looked at her and then at me. She motioned with her head toward the classroom.

He waited a few seconds and then, almost as if to himself, said, "No." He walked away after nodding at the two of us. I gave Dou a non-committal nod and walked back into the classroom. I was very careful during that brief exchange among the three of us not to show any allegiance to either "side."

The meeting between Li Peng and the students on the hunger strike in Tiananmen was televised. Everyone watched. The wavering between pro-student and pro-government news reporting was still in the air. In Wuhan everything blended into a swaying haze: support, rejection of support, a sense of the thrill that integrity might win out, an overwhelming fear that all demonstrators would be killed, and a sense of futility for even thinking of or hoping for change.

Amidst all the flurry, thesis direction continued. One day Matthew, the senior writing on solitude, asked me about God. He said he'd never heard the word "God" until he was in high school. We talked about God, and he asked me if I was a priest. I told him I was. He had many questions, and, as we talked, he said that much of the material we had read and discussed in class all year was beginning to make more sense to him. He said it all connected with his childhood when he would read alone much of the time. His parents lived away from home, and he had to walk a long distance to and from school, so he spent much of his time by himself.

He was deeply appreciative to have had the opportunity to gather his thoughts on solitude for his thesis because he realized how precious and important a part solitude had always had in his life. He said he had always carried it with him and he always would. He wasn't bothered by loneliness because he had his solitude—so different from loneliness.

Interwoven in the frenzied tapestry of those weeks were both the demonic and the beatific. The threat of the government moving in was always in the air no matter how euphoric certain day-to-day events were. I would go to bed remembering Eddie's "green," Norie's "white Yulan," Flora's philosophy of "laughter/tragedy," Madame Fei's desire to provide interesting courses for the students, Lucas's brightness, and Yegudkin's having been thrown onto a railroad car, shot and left to die. I was afraid for all of them. Their appreciation of the void and how it brought them to the threshold of the liberating mystery was also bringing with it the terror of the roofless universe. Could they, could I, embrace the two-fold awareness and "play like Yegudkin?"

"Everything else is only
the framework for the gaze..."[9]

The flurry continued with greater intensity: news reports from the B.B.C., the V.O.A., Radio Australia, or Radio Finland—anything that we could receive at any time of the day or night was our lifeline to the truth. In the meantime, the seniors were getting and missing job opportunities, Mrs. Liang was preparing to move out of her apartment, teachers were wondering about when and how we would schedule final exams for the semester, Madame Fei wanted to know what courses I wanted to offer in the autumn semester, and thesis direction continued.

We then heard that the citizens of Beijing had banded together to keep out the troops sent by the military into Tiananmen Square. Rumors were mounting. On May 30th when the Goddess of Democracy was erected in Tiananmen Square, things in Wuhan began to change visibly. I saw people standing in line to buy rice and oil. I was told this was a bad sign—people stock up on staples because they fear military trouble. The government would soon crack down because they had long been wanting to. The participation of workers in the demonstrations had been too threatening for too long a time. The rumors that Deng Xiao Ping had been in Wuhan twice during the democracy movement made more sense to people now. Wuhan, because of its central location, had been the place from which military maneuvers had been coordinated in the past. People were certain the government had had enough.

I went to bed at 2:00 A.M. on the morning of June 4th, waking up to hear that the worst of what we had feared had happened. Numbness set in and then fury and then fear and then a not-knowing-what-to-do. Old Guo arrived at the apartment and was followed by students. We were glued to the shortwave radio. We knew that the world knew what had happened. Some students had brothers or sisters in Beijing. We had no idea of how many people had been killed. Mao's old motto that "Power comes out of the barrel of a gun," incredulous as it seemed to me, was being played out.

The Gang of Four and several other seniors stayed at the apartment almost the whole day. We made tea and coffee and sat and listened to the radio and expressed outrage—all in slow motion; the day was surreal. In the dining hall, everyone was silent and there was a palpable sense of outrage coupled with shame. Several people on campus said this was worse than the Cultural Revolution—Chinese randomly killing their own. Conversation was in bits and pieces that day.

I was reminded of the morning my father died. We left the hospital, went home and washed and got ready to go to the funeral home to deliver the obituary and select a coffin. When my mother and sister and I returned home, half of our relatives were there. Cars lined the street, and everyone had brought food. We talked and ate and acted as present to each other as possible, but everything in our lives had changed and would never be the same again. Here too, nothing would ever be the same.

George and I were told that most of the students other than the seniors would be leaving the school within a few days. The seniors had to stay to get their diplomas and job assignments and to have their personal files finalized by the university. We heard on the V.O.A. the next day, Monday, that there was still shooting in the streets of Beijing. The possibility of civil war was on everyone's mind.

George and I decided that we would wear black or white that Monday, June 5th. (White is the traditional Chinese color of mourning and black, it was known, is the West's). I wore a long black shirt and went to the department office to ask if we teachers were to report to the classrooms as usual. It was a foolish question, but I wanted an excuse to go to the office. On the way I met vice-director Dou. She smiled and asked, "Why are you wearing black?" Without a moment's hesitation, I responded, "Why are you not wearing black?" and kept right on walking. When I got to the department office, Dou was already there. She must have gone up another staircase, and quickly. I asked my foolish question of the office secretary and Dou answered, "In a few days everything will be peaceful," and smiled again. I looked her in the face and said, "God doesn't know what peaceful is right now."

I felt the visit to the office was futile and wanted to get back to the apartment in case any students came to visit. I met Mrs. Liang on the stairwell. She expressed great sadness and asked how this could happen. Then she said she hoped my mother wasn't too worried. My mother! I hadn't even thought of her. She must have been frantic.

At lunch that day George and I speculated on what might happen next. It was just that—speculation. For the past two weeks George and I had been listening together to the shortwave reports every night after the students left. I'd go to his place or he'd come to mine. That Monday, we listened to the B.B.C. after lunch, when the transmission came in most clearly. Shooting was still going on in Beijing, there were reports of an impending civil war, and foreigners were being urged to leave China.

The next morning, Tuesday, June 6th, I went to our campus Foreign Affairs Office and asked to place a call through to my family. No luck—the lines were jammed. I asked about my passport situation. The deputy director suggested I call the American Embassy in Beijing. A woman answered. I told her my passport was in Beijing. Saying there was still shooting in the streets, she recommended against having someone go to Beijing to try to get the passport. She added that if civil war broke out, I should get as far south as possible and talk my way across the border into Hong Kong. I told her it sounded like a John Wayne movie. She said, "That's about what it is at this point." The deputy director called the Hubei provincial government to see if I could leave the country without a passport. Negative.

Before I left the Foreign Affairs Office, the deputy director said there was concern about George. His age and his blood pressure and the uncertain political situation had them worried. They wanted him to leave the country as soon as possible. I told the deputy director that George was fine and calm. He said they had seen his physical report and were aware of his high blood pressure and the medication he was on. They feared his medication might run out and wanted him to leave because of his age and the situation.

I knew well that the deputy director admired and respected George and that he was genuinely concerned for him. I asked the deputy director to let me handle it. If George felt they were worried about him, he'd be hurt and angry. The deputy director understood. Everyone knew of George's independent, stubborn streak. I explained that I would talk with George when I thought the time was right.

George wanted to know about my passport situation, and I told him. He was very concerned. We had meals as usual, and the seniors came to visit us as usual. Several juniors stopped in to say goodbye. The one who visited on Wednesday afternoons was in tears as he said, "I am worried for my country." It was all so very sad.

My dry little sisters and Matthew, who had written his thesis on solitude, arrived one night to cook several of my favorite dishes. They had a gift for me—a beautiful set of carved Buddhist prayer beads. They invited Lucas for supper too. It was an enjoyable evening, especially in the context of all that had been happening. The looks on the seniors' faces were filled with worry as they communicated in writing with Lucas that night. We all wondered about China's future and how it would affect a bright child such as Lucas.

The news report that night showed film footage of soldiers who had been killed or injured during the student "turmoil" as it was now called. The soldiers of the Peoples' Liberation Army were being made to sound like heroes. One of my dry little sisters shouted at the television, "You all can go to hell!" Then she looked at me and cried, "Even if you can return for another year after this tragedy, don't come back! A country that kills its future does not deserve to have foreign teachers come!"

I tried telephoning my family every day with no success. We had heard that a telephone transmitter had been burned down in Shanghai. Tensions were mounting. An announcement on the V.O.A. stated that a chartered plane was coming to Wuhan to take all foreigners out of the country and recommended that we pack one suitcàse and take our passports. George was worried about my still not having my passport and said he would not leave without me. There was no possibility that either I or a Foreign Affairs Office staff member could go to Beijing to try to get my passport; it was still too dangerous to risk going. I knew I would have to approach George on leaving without me. The deputy director had been pressuring me to talk with him.

Finally, I hit upon an idea. I told George that I could use his June 22nd ticket to Hong Kong and perhaps the Foreign Affairs Office could get him an earlier one. We all knew that tickets were not easy to come by and that chartered planes were being sent by the United States and Canada not only to get foreigners out but also to alleviate the ticket shortage. George adamantly refused. He would not leave the country without me. I badgered him and said at least I would be sure of having a ticket for June 22nd and would most likely have my passport back by that time. He knew I had a point. I asked him to think about it, as time was a concern;

the longer he waited to make a decision the more difficult it would be to get him an earlier ticket for Hong Kong.

Later that day, George came to my apartment and threw his June 22nd ticket on the table. "Goddamn it! Take it!" he said without looking at me. I was grateful that George would be leaving without discovering that people were worried about his age and the state of his health. The Foreign Affairs deputy immediately got George a ticket for June 13th.

On June 10th a Maryknoller from Hong Kong telephoned. Speaking very slowly and clearly, he proceeded to tell me everything that had happened in China from June 4th on. I looked at the telephone as if to say, "No kidding!" I thanked him for calling, told him we knew everything from the V.O.A. and B.B.C. broadcasts, asked him to telephone my family, and told him that George would be arriving in Hong Kong on June 13th.

I finally got through to my family on June 12th. My mother was so upset that she seemed calm. I assured her and my younger sister that I was fine and was just waiting for a plane reservation. They knew I would be home for the summer and that I had been invited back to Wuhan for another year. I asked them not to talk about specifics, as the phone might be bugged. My mother cleverly said, "You have a big and beautiful bridge in Wuhan don't you? It can hold many people for a long time—like three days." The students were so proud that my mother had seen our bridge in her living room! My mother and younger sister spoke with my little sisters. I was thankful to have spoken with my family. I did not tell them that my passport was in Beijing.

On the evening of June 12th the students at our university held a memorial service for those killed in the massacre. The service took place in the university square. On the same evening, before the memorial service, the university officials, the Foreign Languages Department heads, and the staff of the Foreign Affairs Office held a farewell dinner for George and me. Everyone knew George would be leaving the next morning. Just as we were walking into the special dining room where the dinner was being held, the deputy director told me that a Foreign Affairs staff person was being taken to the airport at that time to go get my passport from Beijing. I was both relieved and fearful for the man who went. I knew his wife and son.

George and I wondered if any mention would be made of the Tiananmen massacre during the toasts that were certain to come during the dinner. The vice-president of the university toasted the two of us. He was a gracious and refined man. He profoundly thanked us for our teaching and our friendship during the year. Then he said that the recent misunderstanding between China and America would soon be reconciled and that nothing would interfere with the friendship between our two countries. At least he acknowledged June 4th, but a "misunderstanding"?

Immediately after the dinner, George and I went to the memorial service. Everyone still at the university was there except for a few teachers. I knew that the students had been making white paper flowers, a symbol of mourning, all afternoon. The flowers were hanging on the trees in the courtyard; it was oddly beautiful. As soon as George and I arrived, someone gently took us by the shoulders and scooted us off to one side. The man who did this was a close advisor to the president of the university. We had met him once or twice at important ceremonies during the year. He was a quiet and gentle man. He asked that we not be seen in the campus square. He said, "No one knows how this will turn out."

I said to him, "Everything seems quite orderly and calm here."

He replied quietly, "I am referring not only to this ceremony." I knew he was concerned for us. As he guided George and me to the side and rear of the gathering, he motioned with his eyes to the top of the administration building. I saw a few people standing up there. I would learn when I returned in late August that they had been videotaping the entire service to use in rooting out the students leaders at our university.

The ceremony was somber, quiet, and respectful. George and I were proud of the way the three students who conducted the ceremony presented their testimonies. One of the students conducting the service was a sophomore woman whom I'd taught in the writing and conversation classes. She carried herself with dignity and was most articulate.

After the three students had spoken in a ceremony lasting about fifteen minutes, the vice-president who had toasted George and me at the dinner that evening went to the podium. He said that he and the university were responsible for the safety of those students still at the university. He pleaded that the students confine their expressions of grief to the campus grounds and not venture out onto the streets. He received a heartfelt and full round of applause. The ceremony ended with everyone walking away in silence. That night our students walked throughout the campus; we could hear them softly singing "The Internationale."

The next morning the Foreign Affairs Office staff, the department heads, the senior class and I gathered at George's apartment. The mood was somber as George smiled his goodbyes and shook hands with each person. I watched him closely; I knew his heart was aching with concern and fear for the future of these people and the country he loved so deeply. I also felt heartbroken that he would not be able to return in the autumn to teach.

The Gang of Four and a few men from the senior class got into the van. I sat next to George and, as we drove, conversation in the van was mostly awkward small talk. The usually crowded streets were almost empty. At the airport, we could see that several foreigners were departing. There was a flurry of activity as we unloaded George's many bags from the van. He said goodbye to those who had come with us, and then I accompanied him into customs as did the Foreign Affairs Office deputy director who respected George as a grandfather. When we couldn't go any farther, I hugged George tightly. I heard and felt a short sob as he cried gently. "I don't like leaving you here like this," he said into my ear. I held him and promised that everything would be fine and that I'd see him soon in Hong Kong.

We were all dead silent as we drove back to the university. My year there with George had been like a fable. It had been eleven years since I had worked overseas in Taiwan before coming to China. To have had this year with George was an honor for me.

The Gang of Four and the senior men came into my apartment, and we cooked up some instant noodles. After they left, some junior women came to say goodbye; they were going home. They brought two white paper flowers from the previous night's service. I thanked them. (These flowers are now framed together with Xie Lau Shi's gardenia.) They cried; they had been fervently hopeful during the spring. They were terrified for China's future. We exchanged addresses, not knowing if I would be able to return in the autumn; they doubted that I could. They asked about my passport situation. I told them that a Foreign Affairs staff member had taken a plane to Beijing to get it for me.

That night I went alone to supper. I missed having George to talk with. After George left, the head cook sat with me at every meal. He kept saying that everything would soon be fine and stable. That's what we were hearing on the television news—that the army would soon bring stability back to China's cities and universities. It was stability at all costs. The head cook told me the television news rendition of what had happened in Beijing. He was a good man and wanted to believe what he was told. Of course, I said nothing to contradict him.

That night, June 13th, was the first time the faces of the most wanted student leaders were shown on the news. Each student's full name, date and place of birth, university, height, weight, and any noticeable accent were reported. Rewards were offered for information regarding their whereabouts. It was also reported that the sister of one of the students had turned in her own brother! The students watching the news with me were horrified. Then they quickly concluded that perhaps the sister had done this so that her brother would be treated more leniently. So much of what was happening was "anybody's guess."

At noon on the next day, June 14th, the man who had flown to Beijing to get my passport came to the apartment. He was proud of himself as he showed me the passport. He said it had been quite frightening in Beijing. He had arrived late at night and no one had been on the street. He could hear gun shots every so often. I thanked him very much for going and also for stopping at the apartment as soon as he returned.

I was grateful to have the passport, and yet I also knew it meant that I would soon be leaving. Almost every feeling those days, other than rage and disgust at what had been done in Beijing, was confused, mixed, ambiguous. I didn't know if I would be able to return to China in late August. The next year's contract was signed, the return visa was stamped in my passport, but no one knew or could foresee at that point how relations between China and the United States would evolve. I focused on my immediate feeling: my passport had been returned, I felt unreservedly ambiguous about it, but I was thankful that the man who had gone to get it had returned safely. I was learning to try and take one feeling at a time. It wasn't a good learning experience.

Later that afternoon I went with the deputy director to get my ticket to Hong Kong. He told me that, given the situation in Beijing right now, they would mail me my return ticket to Wuhan during the summer—depending on how "the situation" developed. I was to leave Wuhan on June 17th. I had two more full days there. How very different this was from my first full day in Wuhan the previous September, when I had read "Redemption." Yegudkin had taken the intensified journey of the human spirit. I was hoping that these students and teachers I had come to love and who had given me back my spirit would be safe.

I didn't think of Yegudkin on June 15th or 16th. I was still reading theses and writing my evaluations of them for the seniors. I packed on June 16th. The Gang of Four and several other seniors came to chat. What to say? We laughed at things that had happened during the year. They recalled the red shirt I had worn the first day of classes. They gave their best regards to my mother and sister. Robert came over with some Chinese medicine for my older sister. His girlfriend worked at a medical production plant; she had mailed this at Robert's request. Robert wished my sister well with her cancer. The kindness surrounded me up to the last minute. I was bursting inside with gratitude and tenderness for these students and with rage and fear for what had been done to them, their future, and their hope.

While the students were still at the apartment, George telephoned from Hong Kong. He wanted to know if the passport had come and if I had a flight reservation to Hong Kong. I gave him the information. His voice was filled with vigor and with love. He spoke with each of the students.

On the morning of June 17th, I was writing my last evaluation of the last of the senior theses. My books and belongings were boxed and bagged. They would remain in the Foreign Affairs Office until Mrs. Liang's apartment was renovated and I returned. Madame Fei, the curriculum director, bicycled over from her home. She brought a wicker purse for my mother. She asked me what book I wanted her to have copied for a novel reading course she and I had discussed and arranged for the autumn term. I told her that I thought the book and the film, *Sybil* might be interesting for the students, since it would also follow up on the psychology material we had covered. The book, which I had purchased in Hong Kong, was in one of the boxes. I took it out and gave it to Madame Fei, and she promised she would have it ready for September.

She had tears in her eyes. I did too. I hugged her, thanking her for her gift to my mother and for having the book copied. She nodded and smiled. In a flash I remembered her prophetic suggestion to begin teaching with the last story of the second volume. If only she knew the wisdom of her suggestion and where it had brought me. I looked around the room, taking in the people who were there that morning. I wondered if I would see them again and if they would be safe.

The seniors were waiting outside. I said goodbye to each one—crying and laughing. I didn't know what to say. The education officer came. He shook my hand, looked me in the eyes, and said, "Thank you for being with us." He was the man who had made the rounds of the classrooms during the month of May. I had never spoken to him before, but we had seen each other at various functions during the year. He was also at the June 12th memorial service.

The Gang of Four, some senior men, and the deputy director of the Foreign Affairs Office went to the airport with me. As soon as the van started moving, I started crying. When we approached the front gate, I saw Mrs. Liang walking up the road. I asked the driver to stop the van. Then I reached out the window and we grabbed each other's hands. I promised I would see her at the end of August. She said, "Good," and smiled into my eyes. I wondered if I would really ever see these people again.

We finally got to the airport. I hugged everyone goodbye. We all cried. While I was moving along the walkway into customs, divided from the airport waiting area by a wall of vertical iron bars, my dry little sisters reached through. We grabbed each other's hands tightly. I saw their faces behind those bars as I walked into the customs area. It struck me as so horridly appropriate that in my last mental picture of them they would be their gazing out from behind bars.

I got through exit customs and sat in the passengers' waiting area. I wanted to cry but couldn't. No, it was not that I couldn't. I could have, but I didn't. I don't know why. Maybe I was afraid that if I started I wouldn't stop. Maybe I wanted to wait until I was alone. I don't know.

These people had so graciously given back to me everything that I had thought would hurt too much. They had brought me back to the rear, right-hand side pew of St. Mary's. They gave me back my spirit, and now it seemed that theirs was threatened into submission. Seeing my little sisters gazing out from behind those bars into nothing was so sad.

Remaining at the gateway to the void is the vocation of every human being. In order to remain faithful to the people I met in China and not to betray either them or what they brought me back to, I try to remain at the gateway to the void—maintaining my gaze toward God in a roofless universe.

Their song, similar to that of the untrapped hawk let loose when Yegudkin played the new French horn, would continue to be sung. These students had sung all year—of longing, hope, fear, trust—of everything that bespeaks the human. Their song would ring more beautifully coming as it did through souls present to the void and gazing out into it.

Our green had been called forth. I arrived at the Hong Kong airport. When the automatic doors opened into the arrival area, I saw two arms go straight up in the air. It was George. He hugged me tight. He understood it all.

5

"NO ONE EVER TREATED US SO GENTLY AS THESE GREEN-GOING-TO-YELLOW"

Cradling the Void

These Green-Going-to-Yellow

This year,
I'm raising the emotional ante,
putting my face
in the leaves to be stepped on,
seeing myself among them, that is;
that is, likening
leaf-vein to artery, leaf to flesh,
the passage of a leaf in autumn
to the passage of autumn,
branch-tip and winter spaces
to possibilities, and possibility
to God. Even on East 61st Street,
in the blowzy city of New York,
someone has planted a gingko
because it has leaves like fans like hands,
hand-leaves, and sex. Those lovely
Chinese hands on the sidewalks
so far from delicacy
or even, perhaps, another gender of gingko—
do we see them?
No one ever treated us so gently
as these green-going-to-yellow hands

fanned out where we walk.
No one ever fell down so quietly
and lay where we would look
when we were tired or embarrassed,
or so bowed down by humanity
that we had to watch out lest our shoes stumble,
and looked down not to look up
until something looked like parts of people
where we were walking. We have no
experience to make us see the gingko
or any other tree,
and, in our admiration for whatever grows tall
and outlives us,
we look away, or look at the middles of things,
which would not be our way
if we truly thought we were gods.

—Marvin Bell[1]

Off to the side of the entranceway of the Maryknoll Society headquarters in Ossining, New York, there is a gingko tree. It stands
majestic with its branches layered one upon another, reaching
straight up to the sky. It isn't spreading out much, just pointing
and growing upwards. The gingko is native to China and is the
only tree left of a large family of trees that grew thousands of
years ago. It looks just the same today as it did thousands of years
ago when it grew in the forests of ancient times.

"Well, that's enough for today..."

I remember once when Brother Thaddeus, who knew and respected nature, took me into a small cove of bushes behind the gingko.
The tree seems not to pay any attention to what lies beneath it as
it stretches upward. Yet there, underneath the gingko, were budding gingko trees. Thaddeus smiled as if to say, "See...? Nothing
goes uncared for in nature."

Even though the gingko has taken root in countries throughout the world, books about trees always mention that the gingko is

native to China. It strikes me as I look at the gingko at Maryknoll that it's a misfit here; its home is in China. I wonder how this tree would feel if it were transplanted back there now. Does it remember China after all these years? Would it remember Maryknoll? Would the transplanting evoke its memory?

When I first went to Maryknoll from Pittsburgh to begin teaching, I left behind with friends a Christmas cactus that I had gotten when I first went to Pittsburgh five years earlier. It bloomed twice a year—in December and again in March. When I returned to Pittsburgh in February to submit my dissertation, I got the plant and brought it back to Maryknoll. I thought for sure that the car trip to Maryknoll would throw the plant off cycle.

In late March when the plant came ablaze at Maryknoll, I called Brother Thaddeus into my office to see it. The crimson flowers looked like a fountain of fire. I told him that I thought the plant wouldn't bloom twice this year because of the cold trip from Pittsburgh. As we walked toward the library he responded, "Oh, yes, some plants bloom best when they're under shock. There's one flowering tree that blooms only when an ax is taken to its bark. Beautiful flowers!"

"Really...?" I said. "Just like people—sometimes our best comes out under pressure."

He looked at me, smiled, and said, "That's right. Well, that's enough for today," and he walked into the library to read the newspaper.

Bowed Down, Stumbling, Reminded to Look Up

I saw the same Christmas cactus at my mother's apartment the summer I returned after my first year in Wuhan. The cactus was thriving. My mother said it had bloomed for her that Christmas. My family had seen all the news reports on the democracy movement, saying that everyone in the States had been glued to the coverage for nearly two weeks running. They wanted to know everything and, of course, if I could return.

My family was managing to carry on. I felt left out of the year's time with them. It seemed they had gone through the holidays and days ordinary in a way that made my father's absence more a part of their lives. For me, it was very odd to be home without him there. They were carrying on with the felt and seen holes in their hearts. I was too, but my carrying on was different from theirs.

I visited my younger sister. She met me at the airport and I stayed with her a few days. She understood how I felt almost without my needing to say anything. I visited my father's grave and spoke with him, recalling with him the people I had come to know in China. I visited my older sister and her family in Virginia. I walked through Washington, D.C. Seeing the Lincoln Memorial and the symbols of Western democracy reminded me that our form wouldn't likely be assimilated into China, nor should it be.

Worry erupted at unpredictable times. I still didn't know if I could return to China. I felt as if I were looking at everything through thick bottle-glass. Watching the videotapes and reading the news articles about China that my family had saved for me brought back memories of watching the news and listening to the V.O.A. and B.B.C. with the students in China.

My mother asked me to speak to her senior citizen group about China. They were extremely attentive and concerned about the students there. The care people showed and expressed with regard to the students reminded me of the summer my father was dying and we learned of my sister's cancer. Grave expectations wafted in and through the ordinary air we breathed. It was the same in the summer of 1989.

Communications from China accentuated the situation. George wrote from Hong Kong, filling me in on the most recent rumors there about China. Joseph wrote, signing his letter, "Your little Chinese friend." Several seniors wrote also, saying everything was back to "normal" in China. I knew they couldn't write in detail because of the possibility of the mail being inspected. I was grateful to hear from them, of course, but their letters, the care of people at home, and my family's different-from-my-way of living without my father all served to remind me that I was "out of it" both in China and in the States.

On July 12th I received a telephone call from the New Jersey office of Air China. They had received my return ticket to Wuhan, mailed by the Bureau of Building Materials in Beijing. I was elated!

Immediately, I started preparing courses for the autumn term. I bought *Sybil* and started reading it again. I got conversation tapes, books on poetry, short stories, magazines on movies and soccer and basketball. I planned which films I could use and how I could incorporate them in the family psychology and American literature courses. Then the thought struck me: What if I am not allowed to teach content courses and can teach only grammar, conversation, and listening? After a brief interior pause, I knew I didn't care. I wanted only to be back there with them.

I visited my father's grave again before leaving my hometown. I knew he blessed my return. In a year's time I had come to see more and live more with the extremes of life. I no longer wanted to escape. Knowing this, I wasn't sure how to live with the uncertainties. Strange as that sounds, it was only once I knew I could return to China that I realized I wanted to choose where I would live out this renewed awareness. The uncertainty of not knowing if I could return to China had been nearly unbearable to live with. That had bowed me down—the not knowing if I could return.

Once I knew I could return, I realized that being bowed down had reminded me to look up. I prayed in my not-knowing. I prayed that if I couldn't return, the students would be blessed with all their hope and courage and defeat—that they not be bowed down and forget that the bowed-downness itself is an entrance-way into the void—that the void is the look-out into the remembrance that they can "play like Yegudkin." Then I remembered what the students had said about the crises in life: only in hindsight are we able to see what we can and have learned through them. My being bowed down in not knowing had evoked my looking up through the void to God.

Being able to return was a gift, beyond my control. I accepted the gift with gratitude.

Seeing the Gingko

My younger sister drove me to the airport. I arrived in China at about 11:00 P.M. One of the previous year's seniors was now working in the university's Foreign Affairs Office. He and Matthew met me at the airport in Beijing. It was wonderful to be back! As we drove to the hotel in Beijing, I watched for signs of everything and anything. Life seemed to be going on as usual. We were stopped by security police. They looked into the car, checked identifications, and let us continue.

When we got to the hotel, I unpacked my carry-on bag and gave my two former students gifts of cigarettes and candies I had brought with me from the States. They gave me some Chinese cigarettes and dried fruit. We chatted about their classmates—who got what job. We went to bed with no mention of June 4th.

The next day Matthew and I had a chance to talk a bit. He said his solitude was still with him. I asked him how the summer had gone. He had had a vacation with his family and had then come to Beijing where he was now working. He told me that all students and work units throughout the country were required to attend political study classes each week. There was a campaign to revivify Marxist-Leninist thought, and Mao's thought was also being taught and widely publicized. The efforts to find the student leaders of the democracy movement were still in full swing. There was talk of executions of the movement's leaders. He asked what I'd seen and heard in the States, and I told him. Matthew assured me that everyone knew how to handle things. I thanked him for coming to meet me at the airport. It was a gesture I would always remember.

The next day my former student working in the Foreign Affairs Office and I took a sixteen-hour train ride to Wuhan. I would be living in Mrs. Liang's renovated apartment. There would also be three other foreign teachers at our university that year. My mind and body were on fast-forward when the train pulled into Wuhan. I couldn't get to the university fast enough. Everything looked the same. People were coming and going as they pleased.

We arrived at the apartment. It was beautiful! All painted and clean and more airy. The other staff from Foreign Affairs came to visit with my bags and boxes. It was wonderful seeing the deputy director. Of course, he asked about George. I was told that classes wouldn't start for another two weeks since the students had to make up missed class time from the previous semester's "misunderstanding." This was the first mention of June 4th.

The students started coming to visit that afternoon. It was as if they wanted to touch me to make sure I was really there, and I wanted to touch them to make sure they were safe. They asked about my family. They told me they'd already begun making up classes from last semester and that exams would be held the following week. I went to supper and saw the head cook who'd eaten every meal with me after George had left for Hong Kong. I saw the man who'd gone to Beijing to get my passport for me. I invited him to the apartment and I gave him the wrist watch my mother had bought for him to show her gratitude. He wore it every day from that time on.

That evening more and more students came to visit. Mrs. Liang came and we hugged each other and rocked. She asked how I liked the new apartment—meaning her old one. I told her it was like being home. She beamed! I went out to greet the retired cadres who were playing croquet. They all stopped playing and we shook hands.

The next day several of the previous year's seniors came to visit. More than half had secured jobs in the Wuhan area. Among those who came was one of my dry little sisters. She hadn't solidified her job yet. After the others had left the apartment she stayed behind. She cried and cried, saying, "Oh, Larry, you did come back." She told me that everyone had been terrified over the summer. Interrogations had started and were continuing full force at each university. She told me to mention nothing about June 4th to anyone. I gave her a carton of American cigarettes to use when she thought best as a "gift" to help with her job assignment.

That night, one of the co-chairs of our department came to visit. This woman knew of my dislike of vice-director Dou. She happily told me that Dou had gone abroad to study for a year! How ironic, I thought, but it would be good not to have to deal with her this year. I was waiting to hear what courses I'd be teaching, but didn't want to seem over-eager.

Madame Fei came the next morning. She had a new motor-bicycle. I almost fell over myself running down the stairs to meet her at the door. How we hugged! She had brought a pile of papers and books with her and motioned for us to go upstairs to the apartment. When we got inside, she happily pulled out a list of the courses I would be teaching: novel reading and advanced literature with the seniors, American literature with the juniors, film with juniors and seniors, and writing and conversation with sophomores.

Sybil was all printed! She couldn't talk fast enough, and I couldn't listen fast enough. I asked her why I was teaching more courses on literature and told her I had been afraid I wouldn't be permitted to teach content courses. She said, "No, no. We must create more courses to keep the students interested after everything that has happened." She was even more her spirited, loving self. I'd brought her a beautiful silk scarf. Her eyes twinkled.

I was curious as to how the aftermath of June 4th would show itself at the university. So far there had been no visible indications. There wouldn't be any until classes started. I did notice, however, that there was a person seated at every doorway on campus throughout working hours.

The person in the street was the first to feel the effects of the sanctions imposed by the international community after June 4th. I was told that there had been robberies everywhere that summer. Another visible effect of the aftermath was the enforced Thursday afternoon political classes. These classes had been held the previous year also, but attendance wasn't strictly enforced. This year attendance was taken and students and teachers were reprimanded if they didn't attend. Students had to write repeated accounts at different times detailing their day-to-day actions during the fifty days of the democracy movement of the previous spring. Husbands and wives were called in individually so their stories could be cross-checked.

Each university was to be classified by the government—after extensive research, interviews, and written reports were completed—as first, second, or third degree offenders in the democracy movement. Moreover, students within each university were also to be classified—after interviews and written reports—as first, second, or third degree offenders of the government. Penalties would be determined accordingly. There were also rumors that any student who was either an undergraduate or graduate student in the years 1985–1989 would have to spend one year teaching in the countryside to be "re-educated." Several students and teachers told me that if anyone's name appeared on any report or was mentioned in any interview more than twice, that person was called in by the Party leaders and interviewed.

There was a witch hunt on, and it would continue until the government was satisfied that the student leaders had been found. I also heard that the sophomore who had been one of the three students who conducted the memorial service at our university in June had been called in by the university's Party leadership and interrogated several times. She'd been peppered with questions and shown videotapes. They wanted her to give them names of student leaders in the Wuhan area. What I was hearing sounded exactly like the accounts I'd read in books on the Cultural Revolution.

I was told these things by students who'd visit the apartment. I was grateful that they could still come to visit as they wished. They were trustful and careful not to speak too loudly or aggressively. Everyone knew the truth. The television reports and university loudspeaker reports were the Party lies. It was sickening and disgusting to hear the lies over and over again when everyone knew the truth.

Lucas was in good form. He'd started to visit at least once a week. He wrote me a note saying that his father would be coming home to visit soon and he wanted me to meet him. Xie Lau Shi had been away visiting friends. When she came to the apartment, we exchanged gifts. I had bought a gold-plated cross for her. She told me it wouldn't be a good idea for her to wear it around her neck, but that she would cherish it. Joseph came alone at first. I was touched to see him and thanked him for his letter. He had received my response too—with some beautiful stamps I had selected for him. Old Guo started our weekly visits again. I'd brought him some hardcover books that I knew he'd appreciate.

Seeing these people brought into sharper focus the deceit all around us, a deceit that made me even more disgusted because of their goodness. They knew how to play the games of knowing the deceit yet managing to live with it. They seemed not to be bothered by it. Nothing went past them, though. I was more than grateful that they could come and visit and that they trusted me enough to talk openly about their feelings.

Classes were a joy. American literature with the juniors was still my touchstone. "Redemption's" characters were my anchor and my inspiration. A new group of students read about Yegudkin's transformation of suffering, and the message was received by open ears and hearts. Still, there was noticeably less discussion in the classroom this year. The students told me that there were two Party "spies" in each classroom—students either in or about to join the Party. They pointed the students out to me. I knew these people, and I found it hard to believe that they'd report any of their classmates. The decreased classroom discussion proved me naive.

After the first two weeks of classes, Mrs. Liang came running up the stairs to the apartment, shouting my name. I thought something must be wrong. She was carrying the *Chang Jiang Daily,* a newspaper that was circulated all up and down the Yangtze River. Although she was out of breath, she managed to say excitedly, "There is an article about us in the newspaper!"

I had been washing cups after tea with some students, but I stopped and looked at the paper. I could make out some of the Chinese and, sure enough, there was an article about us. Moreover, there was a sketch of the two of us depicting her offering me a plate of steaming food and me accepting it. I had glasses on in the sketch; it looked more or less like me.

Mrs. Liang was thrilled with the article. She gave me her copy of the paper and said she was going to buy more copies—including one for my mother. I thought it must be a "human interest" type of story and didn't pay that much attention to it.

Later that afternoon, Jamie, one of the seniors, came to visit. She asked if I'd read the newspaper article. I said that I hadn't yet and that I would need plenty of help, but that Mrs. Liang had given me a copy. Jamie suggested that I sit down and listen to her read the article.

The headline, in thick Chinese characters, said, "Lei Li Lu and His Chinese Mother." ("Lei Li Lu" was a phonetic attempt at my English name.) The article spoke of the friendship between Mrs. Liang and me, pointing out that we were across-the-hall neighbors and that she gave me *jyaudz* every Sunday. It said she admired my sense of responsibility in teaching and my friendly manner. The article then went on to say that Mrs. Liang had advised me not to believe any news reports I'd heard on the V.O.A. during the democracy movement, and to believe only the government-run television reports because foreign news organizations did not understand the true situation in China.

I interrupted Jamie at that point and shouted, "What? It's all lies!" Jamie continued reading. Mrs. Liang was quoted as saying that I had been grateful to her for telling me the truth. She said she had advised me to go to class every day and encourage the students to continue doing their school work. The article concluded with the account of my having stretched my hand out the van window on the day I left for Hong Kong and promising her I'd see her at the end of August. Then there was one final lie: the article said I had told Mrs. Liang that I was going to look for a teaching position in her home province because I wanted to live in the homeland that had produced such a wonderful Chinese mother.

I was devastated! How could Mrs. Liang tell such lies? She must have sought out the reporters to do this article. I felt hollow knowing that I had been used and betrayed by this woman. I told Jamie that I had never called her "mother." What a limp retort to the lies written in that newspaper. Then I realized and said to Jamie, "My God, people will be reading this!" Jamie said that most of the students already had and were either furious or so outraged that they had laughed. Students started coming to the apartment while Jamie and I were discussing the newspaper article. They said everyone on campus was talking about it.

I immediately telephoned the Foreign Affairs Office and told the deputy director about the article. He was deeply embarrassed. He came right over to the apartment and explained that this was all Mrs. Liang's doing to make herself look good. I started a string of sentences telling him how I'd never called her "mother," how she had never once said anything to me about the V.O.A., and how the only true things in the article were that we were good friends, that she had given me *jyaudz,* and that I had said goodbye to her from the van. He sat there calmly and said in an understanding voice, "I am sorry that you have had to see this side of China. Mrs. Liang wants to look good and she used you to do it. I will speak with her."

That evening on my way back from supper, two or three people stopped me and said they were surprised I had come back to Wuhan to teach since they'd read in the newspaper that I was going to look for a job in Mrs. Liang's home province. Mrs. Liang came that evening with several copies of the newspaper. She asked me how I liked it; she was all smiles. I said calmly and slowly that it was not a good article. I said I should not be associated in any way with a political situation. I added that any communication about any foreign teacher in China had to be approved by the Foreign Affairs Office of the school or university where the person was teaching. This was the law. I also told her that I had spoken with the deputy director and he would be contacting her. Her face fell. She left without having any tea.

Things moved quickly. The deputy director spoke with Mrs. Liang. He reprimanded her respectfully but firmly. A few days later Mrs. Liang and two women appeared at the apartment door. The women were from the *Chang Jiang Daily*. They said they had written the article at Mrs. Liang's request. Mrs. Liang was completely silent during the visit. They asked if I wanted to write a response. I thanked them and explained that, because of the "misunderstanding" with which the article dealt, writing a response would be awkward. They understood and accepted this.

The entire incident hurt me deeply. I felt dirty. Several people said that I was seeing the underside of China, something that was inevitable in learning about and loving China. I was starting to feel less upset about the whole thing when Madame Fei came to visit a few days later. Madame Fei said that Mrs. Liang's article was "Old China," meaning that people tried to better themselves after some political upheaval by looking good in the eyes of those in power. She said, "When I read that article, I told my husband it was 'bullshit!' I learned that word from watching 'An Officer and a Gentleman.'"

The affair came to an end when Mrs. Liang invited me to her new apartment for *jyaudz*. She'd also invited one of the co-chairs of our department with whom she was friends. I felt very ambivalent and didn't want to go, but not going would have been boldly rude. This was Mrs. Liang's way of apologizing. By that time nearly everyone on campus felt she had used me to her own advantage and that she was wrong to have done so. I went to her home and brought a toy for her grandson. It was quite awkward, and I was grateful that Mrs. Liang had had the wisdom to invite the co-chair of our department.

In an odd way I felt more "at one" with the students through what happened with Mrs. Liang. I had been used as they had been. There was nothing I could do but acknowledge it.

One incident followed another. A teacher in our department, a man to whom I had taken a dislike early on the previous year, came to the apartment. I didn't like him because he regularly announced to the students that he spent one-third of his time on teaching and the other two-thirds in translating books to make more money. His attitude and the fact that he expressed it in front of the students struck me as disrespectful toward them. When he came to my apartment he asked me to join in the interdepartmental singing contest. I told him I couldn't sing—I could only play the trumpet. I thought this would brush him off.

The next day he arrived with a trumpet. Some students were visiting at the time. He proudly said I would be playing the trumpet for the singing contest and our department was sure to win. After he left, the students told me that the contest was being sponsored by the Party in response to the government's mandate that certain patriotic songs be sung at every political theory class and that contests be held. This mandate was countrywide for all universities and all work units.

The following day the choral teacher came and brought music so that I could practice. I told him that I had not been informed that the contest was government sponsored and that, since it was, I could not participate because I was a foreigner. I mentioned that George and I had not participated in any of the student demonstrations last term because as foreigners we could not publicly support or oppose anything connected with the government. This teacher suggested that I reconsider. When I tried to return the trumpet to him, he said I should keep it, because even if I didn't join the contest I might want to use the trumpet for enjoyment.

That night when some students were visiting I told them about what was happening. They asked if the choral teacher had suggested that I keep the trumpet for personal use. When I said he had, they told me to expect more pressure to join the contest. Sure enough—the next morning the teacher I disliked, the choral teacher, and a co-chair of our department all came urging me to join the contest. I gave the three of them the same reasons why I couldn't. They refused to take the trumpet back. That afternoon the three of them plus the department Party secretary came to the apartment. I told the four of them why I could not play. They finally accepted the trumpet. The students took great pleasure in my ability to play the game and win this time.

It was tiring to be exposed to the games and even more tiring to have to play them, but it was worth it, because I was there. The following week I was getting the "thumbs up" sign from several students who'd heard about the trumpet game. They would have wanted to do the same thing, but they couldn't. I wished George had been there so we could have enjoyed these events together.

On the heels of these two events the October 1st holiday approached. The deputy director of the Foreign Affairs Office came to the apartment. He asked me if I'd like to return a third year. He explained that he was asking me himself because they had never had a foreign teacher stay for three years. He wanted to ask me because he thought I would want to return. When I told him I definitely would, he suggested that the two of us go see the vice-president of the university, the man who had spoken at the memorial service.

When we arrived at the vice-president's office, he offered me an American cigarette. I knew this man well from my first year, so I thanked him and said I preferred the Chinese cigarettes I smoked. He broke into a warm smile and said, "Hah! It's good to have an old friend back! I prefer the Yun-nan tobacco myself, but I offer foreigners foreign cigarettes to give them face!"

He then said I was most welcome to return. "But," he added in a more serious tone, "the longer you stay at this university, the more you will be exposed to people like Mrs. Liang and to situations like that happening again." I responded by explaining that I understood and appreciated his concern, but that such situations would not be a reason for me not to return. I told him how impressed I was with the students and the teachers there. He complimented me on my sense of responsibility as a teacher and it was settled. I would return for a third year!

I hadn't expected this at such an early date. The deputy director was clearly watching out for me. He was and still is a good friend. When he writes me letters now, he puts Chinese characters in front of his name above the return address on the envelope; the characters say *"Lau You,"* which means old friend. Such a term of endearment means a great deal.

So there I was, knowing I had more than a year and a half to be with these people I had come to love. In the midst of the lies being broadcast daily on the campus Party line loudspeaker, and in the wake of having lies about me spread up and down the Yangtze River by a person I had trusted, and in the aftermath of

having managed to stay out of the middle of a political songfest—
there I was in China. I had a history with these people, and it was
deepening. Of course, I felt like a foreigner, but at the same time I
knew that the trust that transcends cultural differences was finding
ways to make itself known.

At the same time that I was feeling a deepening trust, doubts
started springing up regarding the "usefulness" of the literature
courses I was teaching. I wondered about the society and life the
students would face after university study. I was learning about
the games they'd have to play and the authorities they'd be dealing with. They had such little chance of prevailing. If I felt so
good and the students felt even better at the "small victory" in regard to the trumpet playing, what chance did they stand in regard
to major battles they would soon be facing? I knew we all have to
play games to fit into society. Truth can be told so rarely in life.
Knowing all this, I was finding myself doubting seriously the use
of my being there and the usefulness of the literature courses. I
was losing the spirit these very people had given back to me one
year ago. I was wondering if they even needed that spirit.

During this period of growing doubt, I found myself sitting
alone one morning trying to pray before the loudspeaker started
blaring the latest statistics indicating how great the soldiers were
or how the economy was growing—all lies. I suddenly recalled
from nowhere a prayer I had discovered years ago when I had
been grappling with doubts. I had been in Pittsburgh at the time
and had just realized what the 340-page rewrite of my dissertation
entailed. I was drowning in discouragement.

When I celebrated Mass, I read the opening prayer of that
week. Part of it was "Let your encouragement be our constant
strength."[2] I thought, "How odd. You'd think we would pray that
God's constant strength would be our encouragement." Then I remember thinking, "No. Jesus knew how it felt to be discouraged.
He lived in this web of fear-producing deceit. He knows how easy
it is to get side-tracked." Then I was struck by the fact that God
wants us to make it, not to get discouraged. And now in Wuhan I
suddenly realized how I was being affected by the lies. I was
being dragged down by the lies surrounding all of us there. I
wanted to be stronger than the lies, but stronger by being more
shrewd, more powerful than the lie-sayers. I wanted to win, to

beat them at their own game. And I realized that I was trying to play the game to win rather than remembering that spirit is more solid than stone.

This was followed by two quiet revelations. It was the thirtieth week in Ordinary Time, and in *The Office of Readings* I found the following on October 31, 1989:

> In this hope, then, let our hearts be bound fast to him who is faithful in his promises and just in his judgments. He forbade us to tell lies; still less will he himself tell a lie. Nothing is impossible for God except to tell a lie. Then let our faith in him be awakened; let us reflect that everything is close to him.[3]

Not only was I a cultural/geographical misfit, I was realizing on more than an intellectual level that I belonged not to this world alone. I had been dragged so subtly into wanting to win at a game that belonged exclusively to a world in which I didn't belong. Pure faith was being asked of me, and it was this to which I was most deeply attracted. It was St. Mary's rear, right-hand side pew all over again, but I got there in a much more convoluted manner this time. I didn't feel laughed at; I felt defensive in a loud, aggressive way. I was deeply grateful to have been reminded of this at that time. The last thing I needed was to get sucked into and entangled in a web of discouraging lies. Were I to do so, the students would have one less person to whom and through whom they could feel some small ray of truth. For them as well as for myself, I was grateful for this slender thread of truth that was stronger than death.

A few days later I was walking through the campus square back to the apartment after a late afternoon class when something caught my eye. Trapped in a low-standing bush under the trees bordering the square was one white paper flower from last June's memorial service. It was there waiting for someone to notice it, and I did! It was the most splendid sight I could have seen! I told the students about it and the next bright sunny day in early November we went to the square to take some photographs. We stood by the bush with the one white paper flower in it—and we left it there so others might see it and remember and be encouraged.

I thought of the gingko standing tall and outliving us. To my knowledge, I didn't look away or at the middle of things. Together with these green-going-to-yellow, maturing into the roofless universe of life, I had my faith in Jesus Who lived this life into its fullness through the void home to God.

Plunged into the Water of Life

With my reacknowledged dependence upon God came a situation and people that dove-tailed my desire to "play like Yegudkin" and the demands that come with it.

The course on *Sybil*[4] was fascinating to the seniors. We would read a section of the book and then watch the corresponding section of the film. It took a while for them to believe that this was the true story of a woman with multiple personalities. The horror and tragedy of this woman's life is difficult for anyone to accept and comprehend. I would refer in class to what we had discussed in the previous term's family psychology course. I wanted the students to appreciate how the persevering care of another person can—with time, love, patience, and a renewed belief in moving from familiar pain to unfamiliar hope—lead to healing.

In listening to the students who came to the apartment to discuss the experience of Sybil and the fidelity of her psychiatrist, Dr. Cornelia Wilbur, I knew that they appreciated the value of "enlightened witnesses." Alice Miller describes enlightened witnesses as those people in our lives who encourage curiosity and spontaneity, who generally believe in and communicate in some manner that we are loved and deserve goodness. While the insights of psychiatry and contemporary psychology might not be common knowledge in China, the truth that enlightened witnesses offer was understood, supported, and received by the students reading *Sybil*. They could see that Sybil's grandmother was that person in her life, and they were willing to reflect upon their own lives and the enlightened witnesses with whom they had been gifted—grandparents, aunts, uncles, neighbors, teachers and their parents. Yet, in mentioning these enlightened witnesses, they also silently acknowledged the "unenlightened" or abusive people in their lives.

In addition, the students were aware of and discussed their own enlightened witness-hood for others. I was grateful that they saw their ability to give this kind of life to others. Always in the back of my mind I remembered that these students would be parents soon. If they could accept their own pain and suffering and see the transforming power of that, they would be enlightened witnesses in their own children's lives.

About midway into the semester, Chen, who was a friend—not a student—I had met during my first year, brought his older brother to the apartment. I welcomed them both, and we had a good visit. I did notice that my friend's brother (Lau Da, meaning "older brother") was somewhat nervous. I didn't know if that was because he was uncomfortable with meeting me or if something else was the matter.

A few days later, Chen came alone to the apartment. He asked if I would please talk with Lau Da because since June 4th Lau Da had not been able to sleep and spoke constantly of his anger over what the government had done. Chen told me that Lau Da had even spoken of wanting to inflict harm on his unit leader who was coming down very hard on those in his unit who had participated in the democracy movement. The current investigations, weekly political classes, and suspicion in the air were aggravating everything for Lau Da.

I told Chen that although I was very sorry about his brother's situation, I had to be very careful in doing anything that would jeopardize either myself or the university. I was also somewhat apprehensive that this might be a "set up," a way of trapping me by getting me to involve myself in something relating to the democracy movement. Chen was obviously quite worried about Lau Da. I decided that if Chen came with his brother, I would talk with Lau Da.

And so began weekly afternoon visits with Chen and Lau Da. Lau Da, who was a professional and married with one child, was about ten or twelve years older than Chen. They didn't know each other very well. Lau Da was very open in talking about his feelings and memories. I liked him; he was sincere. He talked about his memories of the Cultural Revolution; Chen himself remembered next to nothing of the Cultural Revolution, because he had been a very young child when it had taken place.

Lau Da recalled how one night his father and other brother were suddenly dragged out into the street and paraded about the neighborhood. Their father was also a professional, and at the time of the Cultural Revolution professionals were scorned by the Party. That night neighbors jeered at his father and brother and threw stones. The shouting and fear and threat of that night had remained with Lau Da all these years.

One week Lau Da brought diaries he had kept since that time and he read to us from them. Chen had no idea Lau Da had diaries. Just the act of having saved them for all these years was itself dangerous. Had they been discovered, the family could have gone through more suffering.

Lau Da would talk extensively and heatedly. Chen sat there with us every week. I just listened to Lau Da and saw how Chen was learning to love his older brother as a person, not just as an older brother. I could see the growing respect and admiration and love in Chen's face and gestures as the weeks went on.

Lau Da spoke of how he longed for a better China where such acts of violence and disrespect would stop. He longed for a China where people could develop the humane philosophies of their rich cultural heritage. He wanted his child to grow up in an atmosphere as free as possible of the fear he had known as a child. I knew there sat before me a man who had hoped, who still did hope, and who had learned the suffering such hope demands. I grew in my respect for Lau Da as his pain poured forth. Gradually, over the weeks and months, he found himself more at peace inside and feeling less insane for feeling, knowing, and believing as he did. He came to see more clearly that it was not he but the situation that was insane.

Much later, Lau Da came to the apartment with a colleague. They talked openly about their feelings for their country. Since the tactics being used to root out the democracy movement leaders were so similar to those used during the Cultural Revolution, I asked them if they saw any change since that time. The two friends looked at each other. Lau Da said that friends would never have talked to or trusted each other then as they did now. He said that something as fundamental to being human as trust had been broken during the Cultural Revolution. I remember clearly how these two friends looked at each other with affection and confidence.

As the juniors and seniors were nourished by the material we were covering in classes, as they absorbed the perennial truths discussed by the authors we read, I realized more and more how great was their need for that nourishment. Much had been crushed on June 4th and its aftermath. I had never lived amidst such lies. What upset me most as a teacher and a human being were the obvious obstacles put in the paths of these young people. It was senseless—and all for control and stability.

I have looked through my *Office of Readings* from those three years in China. When I pray and something strikes me as supportive of my desire to believe, I write the date in the margin next to it. On October 22, 1989, I underlined the following from an anonymous second century author: "They are happy who, putting all their trust in the cross, have plunged into the water of life."[5]

Also written in the margin is the word "Redemption." I thought of the last line in that story: "Then the crowd opened for him and, with the horn cradled under his right arm, his music under his left, he plunged in, starting home." Plunging into death demands the stretch toward the void. The self-giving and self-emptying of the Holy Trinity was in China. The people there were playing like Yegudkin. They trusted what they had learned and knew through having suffered. The trust and the stretch required of them to live in the midst of lies, deceit, and terrible thwarting of spirit made them more human. They mirrored this to me, and I saw the way to God. I was happy.

Cradling Candy in the Void

Before Thanksgiving, two investigators sent by the provincial government moved into George's old apartment. They were part of the nationwide mandate for the second round of investigations into finding the student leaders of the democracy movement. I heard from a student whose family was "in on" things that if any student who was visiting me should start talking about the situation, I should make sure to either put on music or turn on the water faucet. This sounded strange to me, so I asked why. I was told that the investigators most likely had microphones and tape recording devices to get things on me or the students. I sort of laughed, saying it sounded like "007." "Exactly," was this student's response, and he wasn't joking.

The two investigators lived in George's apartment well into the spring. What a contrast it was—to have had kind and loving George live there last year and to have these two men basing their "operation" out of his apartment this year.

These men ate in the same dining hall where we foreign teachers did. The first night they were there, the taller of the two came up to me and said in English, "I hear you speak excellent Chinese."

I stood up, offered him my hand, thanked him, and politely responded that I was sure he was exaggerating, that my Chinese was not that good. I asked him his name and we shook hands. I felt shivers. How did he know I was the one who spoke Chinese? Who had told him? Would this have a negative influence on any of the students? I tried to look calm, but I instantly felt that these men knew how to read faces and gestures.

They were always polite to us foreign teachers. Whenever university administrators or these investigators would come to the dining room for lunch or supper, a metal-framed cloth room divider would be placed around them. The taller man would always announce in a loud voice, "We do not want any special dishes." Saying this covered him for whatever special dishes the dining room staff brought them. The Party had been criticized last spring for corruption and for pulling privilege. The dining room staff was told what to give them (in terms of special or not special). Those who brought out the food would walk past our table, raise their eyebrows, and lift up the dishes loaded with food! We'd wink. Of course the officials couldn't see this as they were behind the room divider.

Tensions mounted with the arrival of these men. Madame Fei and her husband offered our department the use of their video machine and big screen television. They had a multi-system machine, so I could show some videos I'd brought from the States. I requested and received permission from the university authorities to have a Sunday video day for our department. The students were thrilled! We watched "Sweet Dreams," "The Princess Bride," "The Last Time I Saw Paris" (a film adaptation of F. Scott Fitzgerald's short story "Babylon Revisited" which we'd read in class), and "Funny Girl." We were all bleary-eyed from having watched so many films in one day, but it was great fun thanks to the kindness of Madame Fei and her husband. Her enjoyment was in watching the students enjoy themselves.

Christmas was coming. The juniors, who were in charge of the party, decided to have another dance and asked if I could be Santa Claus. Norie and I put together a Santa suit. I had a bright red bathrobe and red pajamas. Norie sewed up the bathrobe to look like a jacket and sewed on white cloth to look like fur. The sophomore men were put in charge of the beard, which they made from bunches of bright white cotton; the sophomore women made the hat and the junior women made Santa's sack. The sophomore men were to come up with a vehicle that could be used to pull Santa around the large student dining hall where the party was to be held. Norie even got some white gloves! We started planning this in early December.

In mid-December I went to the university greenhouse and bought a potted cedar about five feet high. Then I bought colored, blinking lights and the students started making and bringing in ornaments. It was the first "live" Christmas tree they had seen. It was glorious. Everyone came to the apartment and had a photograph taken next to the tree. Mrs. Liang came with her grandson. Xie Lau Shi recalled how there had been a tree each Christmas in the seminary where she had grown up. Lucas's eyes were as bright as the lights on the tree. Madame Fei made red and silver stars and hung them on the tree. Lau Da brought his son over to see it. I loved watching the children's eyes—filled with wonder and amazement.

Planning the party was an unending series of meetings. I felt as if I were back in the States! Should Santa appear early in the evening or at midnight? What games should we play? How long should the dancing continue? Should Santa give gifts or candy? It was finally settled that Santa would appear at the stroke of midnight after several Christmas carols had been sung; the final carol before Santa appeared would be "Silent Night." As soon as "Silent Night" was finished, Santa would come out on a cart attached to a three-wheeled bicycle that people used on the streets to cart vegetables, metal, you name it! Santa would throw candy from his sack as he was wheeled around the border of the dining hall where the students would be standing in orderly fashion. Did anybody believe this possible?

We did a dry run with the costume in my apartment. The beard needed more cotton. The students were unanimous in their insistence that I not wear my eyeglasses. I was just as adamant in insisting that I would. So we compromised and decided to tape white cotton along the upper rims so it looked as if Santa had white eyebrows. I needed two pillows for my stomach and one for my behind. And no one was supposed to know who was going to play the part of Santa! This was even more impossible than asking the students to stand in an orderly fashion when I was to throw the candy.

Two of the Thursday night culture talks were Christmas carol rehearsals. I had mimeographed the words for everyone: "Rudolph the Red-Nosed Reindeer," "Silent Night," "Jingle Bells," "Santa Claus is Coming to Town," "O Come All Ye Faithful," "Deck the Halls," "Silver Bells," "The Little Drummer Boy," and "The Twelve Days of Christmas"—which one of the students had translated into Chinese so everyone knew what it meant! I went out and got tons of the best candy I could find. I felt a little foolish at first—being so excited about it all. But I was! We all needed this after the interrogations and suspicion and tension.

The excitement had been building for almost a month. The night of the party/dance, Christmas Eve, was very cold but without rain. The student dining hall was packed. All the teachers and most of the administrators were there. Most had brought their young children. The dancing was interspersed with games, including a three-legged race for the foreign teachers. It was truly joyous—genuinely a good time. In between the dancing and the games certain classes had prepared performances. It was all moving very quickly, and the anticipation was mounting for Santa's appearance. We could feel it!

At about 10:30 I went to the back of the dining hall into one of the custodian's rooms to change. Three students came with me. In the room was the sleeping custodian. He had no idea of what was going on. Here we were stuffing pillows into red pajamas and putting on a white cotton beard. Norie had done a great job on the jacket, and the beard was full and flowing. We made a black belt out of someone's scarf and put aluminum foil over a cut-out cardboard belt buckle. It was beautiful! We taped the cotton onto my eyeglass rims and put on the hat—tassel and all. I was all ready, and then one student suggested that what would make it absolutely perfect would be a red nose. Off came the hat, glasses, and beard. The custodian—who had by now woken up—got us some red stamp-pad ink and it was on my nose in an instant. Then someone asked how I would get it off! It was too late to think about that.

I was ready to go at 11:15, but had to wait until the stroke of midnight. I suggested that the students who'd helped me get ready go out and dance for a while. They were to return at 11:45. So there I sat with the custodian. He asked me, "Who are you? Do all Americans do this?" I pulled down the beard, and we had a cigarette. I told him how Christmas was similar to the Chinese Spring Festival.

At 11:45 the sophomores backed the three-wheeled bicycle/cart into the rear of the dining hall. It was about three feet off the ground. They helped me climb into the cart—pillows, candy sack, and hat. The closing strains of "Silent Night" sounded so peaceful. There were no lights on except for the one over the tall Christmas tree the students had put up. And then the four hundred people in the dining hall started singing "Santa Claus is Coming to Town" when the lights were flashed on. I was giddy with excitement; I had never been Santa Claus before.

It was pandemonium! Instantly the students rushed forward. The last thing I remember saying that I thought had a chance of being heard was asking the sophomore who was peddling the cart if he knew where he was going. He nodded and started. The surge of shouting and jumping and cheering students and teachers came toward the cart like a tidal wave. I immediately fell backwards and felt hands propping me back up. I think we got about one-quarter of the way around the dining hall. So much for the orderly standing along the border.

I was throwing candy and waving, and I think got out a few "Ho, Ho, Ho's!" Then the bicycle was stopped by the onrushing crowd. Everyone was screaming, laughing, and reaching for Santa! People started jumping onto the cart. All of a sudden Travis, a tall junior, was up on the cart with me. He was trying to keep people from getting on the cart.

Travis had been suffering recently from very bad headaches —to the point of vomiting. He had missed several days of classes. He had just had an eye examination and had been given a new prescription for his glasses. In the melee on the cart, Travis lost his new glasses. He shouted over to me that perhaps the glasses had fallen into the candy sack. As I reached way down into the sack, the crowd let out a swooping yell, since they thought I was going in for more candy. I started yelling, "His glasses! His glasses!" Madame Fei saw my face from the side of the room where she had been announcing songs. I heard her voice in the midst of the crowded, screaming, reaching chaos, "Calm down now. Santa is getting angry!" I recognized students' faces—and I tried to tell them to look on the floor for Travis's glasses. Impossible!

I attempted to pinpoint where we were in the dining room so I'd remember where Travis's glasses had fallen. The crowd looked like a massive dragon stuck in molasses trying to follow the cart which couldn't be seen and wasn't moving. At that point, a senior woman jumped onto the cart. She was smiling and waving like a beauty queen. I cried out to her as I threw the last of the candy, "Get the hell off of here! You'll be crushed!" She looked over and beamed, "Yes!" So much for her listening comprehension.

The entire event lasted no more than five minutes. I loved it all! I jumped off the cart and landed in a mass of hands. Suddenly I found myself in front of one of the teachers in our department. I'd promised her a dance. With everyone walking around us pulling at Santa's beard (which miraculously stayed on), she and I danced to no music!

It was an ecstatic Christmas season that culminated on Christmas Eve. In that dining hall was everything human, everything that responded to the divine appeal.

Unbelievably to everyone, Travis's glasses had landed at the feet of one of the foreign teachers—unscratched!

Grace Does Not Disjoin, It Integrates[6]

Exams went very well. The juniors' essays for the American literature course met all my expectations. Since I'd read their poetry in October 1988, I knew these students were ready to express their truth once they were asked. Similarly, the seniors responded well to the truths revealed in *Sybil*.

One of the seniors said to me once, "You are very demanding of your students." I told her I knew that. She asked why I was so demanding. I didn't have to think before answering, because I knew why: a good teacher is always demanding, because a good teacher looks for indications of wisdom in his or her students and, trusting those indications, offers opportunities for the students to express it. It feels demanding because of the trust the teacher has in the students. It feels demanding because the students might not know they have that wisdom within. Looking back on the essays I had assigned and the questions I had asked of the students during those three years, I could see I was demanding. I knew I trusted them.

The students gave me gifts galore for George when I left for Spring Festival vacation in Hong Kong. George, Tom, and I ate and shopped and enjoyed each other's and Hong Kong Maryknoll's company for the three weeks. George was teaching English in a prison and also doing some tutoring. Of course, he was full of questions about all of the students; he wanted to know where the graduates from the previous year were working.

When I told him about Mrs. Liang, he winced. I went on to describe how she had invited me for a *jyaudz* reconciliation meal and how she and her grandson had come to the apartment to see the Christmas tree. "Good, kid," he said. He told me that being in Wuhan had been his best year in China. My heart was full when I heard that.

I chose films to take back to Wuhan that would support the truth we had been discussing in classes and that merited confirmation: "Amadeus," "Tender Mercies," "One Flew Over the Cuckoo's Nest," "Moonstruck," "Rainman," "Now, Voyager," "To Kill a Mockingbird," "Nuts," "My Left Foot," "The Glass Menagerie," "Cat on a Hot Tin Roof," "A Streetcar Named Desire," "The Great Santini," "East of Eden," "Driving Miss Daisy," "Tootsie," "The Way We Were," "Moscow on-the-Hudson." We also read the plays and watched the film adaptations of "My Left Foot" and "The Glass Menagerie." I used the films during my remaining year and a half in Wuhan. For all of them I typed up detailed accounts which served as our texts for the film course and supplemental materials in the American literature and family psychology courses.

The films were filled with misfits who could "play like Yegudkin." "Moonstruck" was filled with love and death as well as addressing the "bad luck" or fate that is so prevalent in China. Putting up a good fight with fate in the faith and with the insight that comes through acknowledging the terrifying and liberating roofless universe filled our discussions during the remaining time I had with the students.

During my final two years in Wuhan, I was advisor for the students who were writing their B.A. theses on topics dealing with psychology. The themes they wrote about gave them an opportunity to bring together those insights they had evoked, reflected upon, and accumulated during their university years.

One woman wrote on "Loneliness." In the course of our discussions, I asked her to jot down reflections that could be integrated into her writing outline and her main and supporting ideas. In one reflection she wrote the word "something" several times: "When I don't run from the fear of loneliness 'something' happens... 'something' reminds me that I can face my loneliness." I asked her to write more about that "something."

When she appeared the following week, her eyes were filled with something new. "Larry" she said, "could that 'something' be God?" I told her it could and that we could talk about it, but that she had better not write anything about it in her thesis or we'd both get in trouble. I was happy for the fact that something fundamentally human that she was willing to reflect upon had brought her to the threshold of God.

Time and again through ways and people open or closed to the void that waits for acknowledgement of social misfitness and to the mystery that awaits the acknowledgement of the void—I was brought closer to my truth. That in itself gave me inspiration to want to keep "playing like Yegudkin."

There were three incidents that brought my time in Wuhan to a thankful ending that has remained with me and gives me the desire to keep on believing in goodness and truth. The first was one evening when several seniors, who were graduating at the end of my second year there, were visiting the apartment. We were reminiscing about the past two years and one senior said, "You know, we hate you." There was both a joking and a hate-tinged tone to his voice. He went on to explain, "You remind us of things we cannot be or have in China: people of integrity, freedom, choice. You've stressed the importance of learning from crisis, and told us that being misfits is good. These things are not possible here. You never understood."

I was shocked! Could I have been so off-base as to think my trusting in the human mystery was causing them to be frustrated? I remembered having thoughts like this during my first year. They all flashed through my mind as I listened to him. Another senior piped in, "Oh, no. Listening to you talk about these things makes us feel we are not strange for thinking about them and wanting them in our lives. And when you show us how these authors say how difficult it is to try to be honest human beings, we feel the truth too."

A conversation with Dominic, a 1991 graduate whom I'd had in class for three years, was the second incident that gives me hope. About two weeks before graduation he came to the apartment alone. His manner and expression were quite serious that day. He had thoroughly enjoyed the slang class I was asked to teach when he was a senior. His B.A. thesis, "A Psycho-Social Interpretation of Profanity," had been chosen as the best of our department that year and submitted to the Hubei provincial contest to qualify for an award.

The day he came to visit he said to me, "You know, I will become a bastard after graduation." I asked him what he meant. He explained, "I will want to climb high in my working unit; I will want to buy a television for my parents; I will want to compete and be better than others, and I will have to hurt people to do these things. So what is the good of your having been with us these three years and teaching us what it means to be a good human being?"

I was silent for a while, then I said, "You will know that you're becoming a bastard, Dominic, and that's the good of our having discussed these things for these three years. Also, even the fact that you ask this question shows that you are a good human being."

"You dau li...you dau li..." he said. [It makes sense; it is reasonable.]

The third was the following note I received from a 1991 graduate who had been sent to the countryside to teach for one year as a means of being re-educated. This was in response to the democracy movement mandate from the government for all students in university between 1985 and 1989. She wrote to me in the States:

> The working conditions are very bad. However, we must bear it. I learned to fit the new life here quickly, although I'm still a "misfit" in my heart. I tried to find the balance and manage to keep it...I don't want to work here for a long time because I don't have a chance to use what I've learned here. That's very sad, but I'm not depressed.

She would be fine because she knew her heart and was returning to it.

As I look back over the three years in China and see how much came together interiorly for me, I realize it was because circumstances outside of me erupted into disorder and provided the occasion for interior disintegration as well. The exterior disintegration occasioned a felt social misfitness, and the interior disintegration revealed long-held memories of childhood social misfitness. The social misfitness of my childhood had brought me to God Who doesn't laugh. Everything that happened during my time in Wuhan had served to draw me closer to the truth that had originally brought me to that God.

The cultural/geographical dislocations of my foreign missionary vocation, going to and from Wuhan, Hong Kong, and my home in the States all served to bring me back to the gateway to the void.

George died on July 16, 1991, in Hong Kong. After two surgical procedures in the States, he had flown back to Hong Kong to die as close to China as possible. He is buried next to the New China News Agency headquarters—watching all that is going on.

I happened to go to China where the exterior disintegration of the university students mirrored all of mine to me, and I, in turn, mirrored theirs to them. The visits with Joseph, Madame Fei, Old

Guo, Xie Lau Shi, Lucas, Lau Da and Chen, and Mrs. Liang reminded me that "the impact of love comes through small fideli-
ties . . . performed in service to the mystery of the Word."[7]

And, of course, I was Santa Claus for the last Christmas celebration we spent together.

The grace of God integrated all that was disjoined within and
outside of us at that time. And the foundation of truth laid in those
three years, in fable-like, sacramental fashion, remains.

6

"MEMORY LIKE MELODY IS PINK ETERNALLY"

Mirroring the Divine Appeal

> Blossoms will run away,
> Cakes reign but a Day
> But Memory like Melody
> Is pink Eternally.
>
> —Emily Dickinson[1]

It has been five years now since I left Wuhan. Just as Xie Lau Shi holds prominence in my memory because, to a significant degree, she represents and brings forth both my love for the Chinese people and what inspires my vocation as a foreign missioner, so, too, does Flannery O'Connor's short story "A Good Man is Hard to Find,"[2] for the same reasons.

Stretching toward the Godhead
from Social Misfitness through the Void

It was the most difficult story to teach in China, yet it confirmed what all the people and teaching had evoked in helping me remain within both the terrifying and liberating dimensions of the roof-less universe. O'Connor's story validates Yegudkin, Faulkner, all the characters in the stories we had read and in the films we had viewed. The beacon she provides for humanity in this story mirrors the divine appeal in its invitation to stretch from social misfitness through the void toward the Godhead.

The power of this story colored much of the material I presented and discussed with the students. O'Connor cuts through the philosophical, political, social, psychological, and spiritual illusions and blinders that Western culture bandies about to cover over the transcendent nature of what it means to be human. "A Good Man is Hard to Find" both captivates me and serves to validate for me the intrinsic connection between the vocation of foreign mission and what it means to be human.

O'Connor guts the stereotypical notion of misfitness in her story. One of the two main characters is a serial killer named The Misfit. The capitalization of The Misfit's name reveals more than just his name; O'Connor is challenging and taking us beyond our secure understanding of misfitness. For O'Connor, The Misfit represents every human being who evades transcendence. Her Misfit distances himself from those parts of life and the world that cannot be controlled or manipulated into that concrete part of his life that he can control and manipulate. Such a life for O'Connor's Misfit is the daily excuse that passes for ordinary existence but is, in truth, an evasion of transcendence [3]

The life/death/resurrection of Jesus throws off balance everything controllable and manipulatable. Jesus isolated himself from nothing and in everything remembered the invitation of the Godhead and the response of which we are capable:

> For O'Connor...Jesus lived out the total human situation. If the "way to despair" in O'Connor's psychology is "to refuse to have any kind of experience" (*Mystery and Manners*, 78), then Jesus is unalloyed hope in His embrace of whatever life entails. In addition to making the Father's love visible to the world, Jesus is the supreme realization of the human response to the Father's offer. He shows us how to love. Again, as The Misfit says, His example "thown everything off balance."[4]

O'Connor's truth is illustrated in the story in such a manner that the reader cannot forget the ugliness of one who turns away from God for any reason.

The other main character in the story is a pious, manipulating grandmother who lives with her son, his wife, and their two young children in Georgia. The family is planning a motor vacation. Everyone except the grandmother wants to go to Florida; she wants to go to Tennessee. Despite her efforts, including relating a newspaper report that The Misfit has escaped from prison and is headed toward Florida, she fails to get her way.

The family sets out for Florida, but on the way the grandmother remembers an old plantation she'd like to visit and cajoles her grandchildren into pestering their father until he turns around and, after driving back about a mile, turns onto a deserted side road, following his mother's directions. Suddenly the grandmother remembers that the plantation she'd been thinking of is in Tennessee, not Georgia. She twitches with the realization and the family cat she has secretly brought along is startled, jumps out of a hidden basket and onto the father's neck. The car swerves and rolls over into a ditch.

The family pulls itself up, and suddenly the grandmother notices an approaching black, hearse-like automobile. Three men get out, and the grandmother recognizes one of them as The Misfit. In the course of the story, The Misfit has his men take the members of the family, a few at a time, to the woods off the road and shoot them.

The grandmother is left alone with The Misfit. She tries to reason with him, encouraging him to pray, saying that Jesus will make everything all right. She does not truly see The Misfit; she is only terrified and trying to persuade him not to kill her. Suddenly, her fear strips away the pieties which she has used to protect herself from life and she realizes The Misfit's true goodness. She feels a tenderness for him, calling him one of her own babies. She reaches out to touch him, and he, not able to tolerate any tenderness, shoots her three times in the chest.

After I'd re-read the story, I thought over why I had gone to China in 1988. I had wanted not to care. I had wanted to seal myself off from all that could hurt. I had wanted no tenderness. I had wanted to limit myself to grammar, conversation, and anything that had nothing to do with meaning—thus the attraction to Wuhan University of Technology. Looking back now, I see that I was depressed in the clinical sense of the term.

Alice Miller offers insights that support O'Connor's appreciation of the misfit as one who limits himself or herself to what can be controlled or manipulated in life and thereby experiences no vitality:

> The true opposite of depression is not gaiety or absence of pain, but vitality: the freedom to experience spontaneous feelings. It is part of the kaleidoscope of life that these feelings are not only cheerful, "beautiful," and "good"; they can also display the whole scale of human experience, including envy, jealousy, rage, disgust, greed, despair, and mourning.[5]

When I left the States in 1988, I wanted no feelings. I tried to pretend that I had none. Meeting and coming to love the people in Wuhan from that night in early September when Gardner's "Redemption" punctured through my attempt to control and manipulate life, I was welcomed back into life by those people who had the courage to live. None of them—Xie Lau Shi, Eddie, Norie, Lucas, Flora, Joseph, Mrs. Liang, Lau Da, Madame Fei, George, nor those whose hopes had been slaughtered on June 4th—crawled back into the roofed universe. I can see clearly that their breaking through my attempts to keep myself from feeling—from life—connected me to the misfit phenomenon and its cure: turning toward the transcendent through the felt social misfitness that reveals the void that holds the mystery of the Godhead.

Social misfitness is but the gateway to the void. The true misfit is the person who refuses to live with the sometimes frightening yet freeing openness into eternal mystery.

The Architecture of Lives Lived

The people I met and came to love in China called me back to St. Mary's rear, right-hand side pew when, as a fat, laughed-at child, I knew that God did not laugh at me. The architecture had changed: these people had been broken by this life and the roof of their certitude had been ripped off. What they offered in place of the beeswax, the smell of the pews, and the beautiful architecture of

St. Mary's were their poems, their smiles, their fears, their pain, their hopes, and their joys.

They were not concerned about maintaining the delicate, poised position that would deceive them into thinking they could continue to control their lives. They knew they couldn't. The breakthrough into the social misfit's life dissolves the temptation to focus on one feeling or one way of living. It liberates one from needing to control, or to give up responsibility, or to mock those who do not fit in socially. It liberates one from feeling only the terror without the freedom, or being confined to relating only with others who whine about not fitting in socially, or relinquishing any personal desire and following the definition others provide.

Once broken into by the tender acknowledgment that comes through relating with honest people who are both terrified and liberated, misfits' horizons are opened; they can reach through their felt social misfitness toward the transcendent through the void that had separated but now connects. Until this breakthrough happens, social misfits will perceive themselves and life in a stunted manner; they will refuse or be unable to perceive social misfitness as a bridge connecting them to the transcendent, that is, to a life lived more to the full.

As I read the story and reflect upon its implications for myself and for foreign missioners, I cannot help but see the misfit theme as underlying my own journey from the world of a fat, laughed-at little child into the cultural/geographical fringe of foreign mission. Foreign missioners, who are incapable of ever being able to fit in totally to the host culture, are a living symbol of the human condition. The choices they face represent every human being's fundamental temptation to accept or to reject the transcendent dimension in life.

The limiting options mentioned above are doubly present in the life of foreign missioners. Missioners' choices can support or weaken an appreciation of the human mystery because they are public people and also because the vocation itself, to retain its uniqueness and connection to God, must maintain the strongest possible interwovenness with the fundamental human mystery.

The vocation of foreign mission, like any vocation, is validated to the degree that it bespeaks the human mystery. And foreign mission bespeaks the fundamental options open to the universal

social misfitness of all individuals, all humanity. Foreign missioners do not fit in; this is central to their vocation. Therefore, to
some degree, the fundamental human mystery is failed when foreign missioners concentrate on fitting in to the host culture at the
expense of maintaining the uniqueness of their vocation. The foreign missionary vocation is bound up with the lives of the social
misfits of the host culture who mirror to foreign missioners the
foundation upon which their vocation claims its unique connection and contribution to the human mystery.

Swelled with Pain into Candid,
Clumsy Truth and Joyful Compassion

Many of these thoughts have become clearer to me since I left
Wuhan. I need them; I do not have the daily reminders of seeing
Xie Lau Shi, Lucas, Norie, Eddie, Madame Fei, Flora, and Lau
Da, or George who is with God. The memory of these people is
made more alive through understanding O'Connor's insight.

O'Connor's definition of true misfits as those social misfits
who evade the transcendent by focusing only on their inability to
control life fascinates me. I looked up the definition of *evade* and
found: "to escape or avoid by cleverness or deceit." I myself had
attempted an escape through going to China, abusing the very vocation that can support the human mystery by turning toward the
transcendent through felt social misfitness.

The power-holders in China or in any other culture attempt to
avoid the humanity of those to whom they are responsible by
making deceitful promises or ruling through intimidation. Victims
of power-holders can also avoid their transcendent nature by accepting the lies of the regime—accepting to the point of becoming
numbed. Even after oppressive regimes (of any magnitude, from
parents to nations) lose their control through the upsurge of the
human spirit, transcendence can continue to be evaded through a
multitude of escapes such as scapegoating, blame, despair, blind-
ness, or a refusal to take on the burden of freedom.[6] Unless and
until the human spirit along with its fears, hopes, joys, and bro-
kenness that lead to the transcendent is acknowledged and supported, the evasion will continue and escalate.

O'Connor's Misfit wanted certitude, and for him certitude
was an impossibility because he hadn't been there when Jesus
raised the dead:

> "Jesus was the only One that ever raised the dead,"
> The Misfit continued, "and He shouldn't have done it. He
> thown everything off balance. If He did what He said,
> then it's nothing for you to do but thow away everything
> and follow Him, and if He didn't, then it's nothing for
> you to do but enjoy the few minutes you got left the best
> way you can—by killing somebody or burning down his
> house or doing some other meanness to him"...
> "Maybe He didn't raise the dead," the old lady mum-
> bled...
> "I wasn't there so I can't say He didn't," The Misfit
> said. "I wisht I had of been there," he said, hitting the
> ground with his fist. "It ain't right I wasn't there because
> if I had of been there I would of known. Listen lady," he
> said in a high voice, "if I had of been there I would of
> known and I wouldn't be like I am now."[7]

Neither The Misfit nor any of us knows; we are all clumsily
vulnerable:

> The Misfit's need for certitude is a modern misreading of
> faith. Those who were there with Jesus conducted them-
> selves as clumsily as we. They misunderstood him. They
> also deserted him. Only after the resurrection did the dis-
> ciples understand the Word they listened to. The Misfit
> may already be more privileged because the inner mean-
> ing of the Word he hears comes invisibly. Those are
> blessed who believe without seeing. And the comfort of
> love, a small Pentecost, is imminent, but The Misfit
> clings to his autonomy.[8]

When the grandmother reaches out to touch The Misfit, when
she breaks through her own defenses of pieties and personal idio-
syncrasies to see the truth—that The Misfit is all of us—"one of
her own babies"—he shoots her three times in the chest:

Tenderness misfires when aimed at The Misfit, because a person who cannot feel pleasure abhors human contact. The Misfit's dread of human intimacy keeps open the emotional wound of his past. The grandmother's kindness calls to the frightened softling buried deep within the hardened criminal, but he will do anything to avoid facing the vulnerable part of his nature.[9]

The vulnerability in The Misfit's life is traced back to his personal history, and his personal history is the personal history of each human being, namely, imperfect, riddled by sins committed by and against him, and the consequent felt need for protection. The need for protection against sin and imperfection gives rise to the need for certainty. In blaming his mis-timed history, his not having been there when Jesus raised people from the dead and thus not knowing if it is true, The Misfit decides to protect himself by enjoying himself—and his means of enjoyment is a means of self-protection: he kills.

The grandmother also protects herself from her uncertainty. Her means, a feeling of near self-righteousness and scatterbrained bossiness, make of her "Every-grandmother... She obviously works out her life on surfaces, a trait worsened by a sentimental moralism that disposes her to the critical animosity she has received"[10] from her family.

Her trite pieties are as much an evasion of her real self as is The Misfit's cruelty. In the grandmother's case, readers are amazed to learn, birdbrained truisms conceal a loving woman. Her effort to adopt a killer whom society condemns wins a victory. Humility and bare truth invoke a standard for action that brings her assailant to a standstill. The norm is Jesus, Whose name she mutters, and it turns out that the widow pays the ultimate price Jesus paid for love.[11]

When the grandmother's illusions and defenses melt through fear, she sees. In the moment of bare truth facing her and The Misfit she sees through her self-protection and she feels more than fear. She sees that her life has been off-balance. She sees in a way

that The Misfit has always seen. Yet she sees through her awareness of life's off-balancedness—she goes beyond that awareness
to see through her pieties and moralism. The grandmother's face-
to-face encounter with herself through facing The Misfit before
her and the misfit inside herself lifts her self-protection. She recognizes The Misfit as one of her own children, a fellow human
being. She sees clearly and reaches to touch his thin shoulder—to
support him in his humanity.

In an unbalanced, uncertain life, a connection between people
who recognize the truth can lead to mutual encouragement and
support in stretching toward the transcendent. But The Misfit
turns his soul on the grandmother's gesture of mutual recognition.
He remains both a social and a spiritual misfit while she accepts
her transcendent truth as a human being. She is killed, but dies "in
a puddle of blood with her legs crossed under her like a child's
and her face smiling up at the cloudless sky."

> She, unlike the morose killer, finds a way to pleasure by
> becoming a child of love. O'Connor's controversial
> image of the dying grandmother explains the paradox.
> The grandmother squats in blood...Though her cheerful
> expression before ignominious death scandalizes sullen
> readers, we do well to recognize...O'Connor's strategy
> of combating sorrow with exuberance, because a sense of
> humor is an important ingredient of her faith. In the
> grandmother's bearing of The Misfit's burdens, her
> weakness strengthens her to endure her executioner's
> scorn with joyful compassion. With her share in the
> world to come open above her, the lady can beam a smile
> ..."A Good Man is Hard to Find" demonstrates love as
> spiritual identification. Interior resemblance, in turn, lo-
> cates the good woman. In the end, the grandmother takes
> The Misfit as she takes herself, and loves him with the
> humility that allows access to another's subjectivity.[12]

In accepting her humanity and her propensity to be a misfit in
her unique way, the grandmother is open to going beyond her own
experience of fear and means of self-protection. She turns toward
her inner void and finds waiting a mystery that is terrifying but

also liberating. The liberating aspect opens her to reach toward the other as well as toward The Other. In such recognition and acceptance, a burden is lifted, relief is felt, and joyful compassion and the ability to enjoy life rushes in.

O'Connor's story ends with the words of The Misfit. When his prison mates return from having shot the last members of the family in the woods and find the grandmother dead, one of them, Bobby Lee, says to him, "Some fun!" The Misfit responds, "Shut up, Bobby Lee...It's no real pleasure in life." The Misfit, remaining closed and incapable of accepting the universal truth that we are all out of control in the presence of the transcendent, cannot enjoy anything. His energies are completely focused on the lie and the pain.

Yet O'Connor has faith in The Misfit. "The grandmother's gesture...carries so much spiritual momentum that O'Connor envisions a continuation. The seed planted by the old lady's kindness, O'Connor muses, will become 'a great crow-filled tree' that will swell The Misfit's heart with enough pain 'to turn him into the prophet he was meant to become' (*Mystery and Manners*, 113)."[13]

The opposites of cleverness and deceit—which, according to the definition of *evade,* are necessary to avoid—are clumsiness and candor. The effort to control demands cleverness because social misfits want to look as if they fit in. They do not want to appear clumsy. They are deceiving themselves. Once these energies can be candidly released, acceptance of our lot and our truth, namely, that we were not made for this world alone, will transform us into a joined humanity receptive of God's grace. The pain of social misfitness is, thereby, a sacrament—the most direct shunt to God Who expressed the Godhead's desire for open self-giving and self-emptying into love by sending Jesus to show us how the stretch through social misfitness takes us to the gateway of the void where the God Who doesn't laugh awaits.

I need to absorb O'Connor's graced understanding of social misfitness, especially when I am no longer with the living sacraments of Wuhan. When I become over-burdened by exerting too much energy to keep up my defenses, I know that I am, in one way or another, trying to fit in. And I know that fitting in has assumed a value it doesn't deserve.

Then I remember the Christmas Eve celebrations in Wuhan. Their exuberance and joy bring me home again to the truth of my vocation as both human and foreign missioner. Then I am again "green in the green" because "memory like melody is pink eternally." And the divine appeal can resume its mirroring within and among all of us for "twenty minutes, more or less."

NOTES

1. "Where Winds Meet"

1. Anne Morrow Lindbergh, *Hour of Gold, Hour of Lead* (New York: Harcourt Brace Jovanovich, 1973), pp. 180-181.

2. Thomas Merton, *Mystics and Zen Masters* (New York: Delta, 1967), pp. 92-93.

3. Fung Yu-Lan, *A Short History of Chinese Philosophy*, ed. Derk Bodde (New York: The Free Press, 1966), p. 8.

4. David Tracy, *The Analogical Imagination* (New York: Crossroad, 1981), p. 124.

5. Bishop James Edward Walsh, M.M., "Description of a Missioner" (Maryknoll, New York: Development Department, 1976), p. 2.

2. "Where Is Green?"

1. A poem by Eddie, a student in the sophomore writing class, Wuhan University of Technology, Wuhan, Hubei Province, China, fall semester, 1988. Used with permission. All of the works by students cited throughout are used with their permission.

2. John Gardner, "Redemption," in *The Art of Living and Other Stories* (New York: Knopf, 1981), pp. 30-48.

3. John B. Breslin, S.J., "Vision and Revision: Seamus Heaney's New Poems," *America,* December 7, 1991, p. 438.

4. Tracy, p. 124.

5. Oscar Williams, Introduction to *Immortal Poems of the English Language*, ed. Oscar Williams (New York: Washington Square Press, 1952), p. 9.

6. Dag Hammarskjold, *Markings,* trans. Leif Sjoberg and W.H. Auden (New York: Knopf, 1976), p. 131.

7. William Faulkner, "Address Upon Receiving the Nobel Prize for

Literature," in *Essays, Speeches and Public Letters,* ed. James A. Meriwether (New York: Random House, 1965), pp. 119-120.

8. Mary Tkalec in *I Never Told Anybody: Teaching Poetry Writing in a Nursing Home,* by Kenneth Koch (New York: Random House, 1977), p. 67.

3. "...The Fountain-light of All Our Day"

1. The following popular expression of the misfits' way of evoking a truth about ourselves is a monologue performed by Bette Midler (copyright 1977, Divine's Music Ltd., BMI) and is found on *Bette Midler Live at Last* (Atlantic Recording Corporation, New York, 1977, Atlantic Compact Disc No. 81461-2): "I was walking down 42nd Street one day, and this amazing thing happened to me. It was July. It was about 89 degrees. It was hot, hot for New York, you know? And I was walking east, and this humongous person was coming west, and she had this big blue house dress on, peckered all over with little white daisies, you know? She was almost bald, but sitting on the top of her head, forehead, you know, on her forehead, was this fried egg which I thought was really unusual because in New York City the ladies with the fried eggs on their heads don't generally come out 'til September or October, you know? Here was this lady, this demented lady, with a little fried egg on her head in the middle of July. God, what a sight, oh! And ever—ever since I saw that lady, not one day goes by I don't think of her, and I say to myself, 'Oh, God, don't let me wake up tomorrow and wanna put a fried egg on my head. Oh, God...' Then I say real fast, I say, 'Oh, God, if by chance I should wind up with a fried egg on my head,' ('cause sometimes you can't help those things, you know? You can't!) I say to myself, 'Don't let anybody notice.' And then I say real fast after that, 'If they do notice that I'm carrying something that, that's not quite right, and they wanna talk about it, let 'em talk about it, but don't let 'em talk so I can hear. I don't wanna hear it.' 'Cause the truth about fried eggs—you can call it a fried egg—you can call it anything you like—but everybody gets one. Some people wear 'em on the outside...some people...they wear 'em on the inside."

2. William B. Frazier, M.M., "Priesthood and Brotherhood in Maryknoll: Missiological Foundations" (unpublished manuscript, Maryknoll, New York: 1994), especially pp. 11-20; and class notes in "The Liberating Cross," a course offered at Maryknoll School of Theology, fall semester, 1994. In his work, Frazier describes Trinitarian life as love characterized by mutual self-giving and utter openness shared among Father, Son, and Holy Spirit in eternity. The desire of the Godhead to share

that life with human beings in time and history can best be communicated through the utter self-giving that is the experience of death. Biological death as well as the brothers and sisters of death, (e.g., anxiety, loneliness, the felt void), demand a walking into those dimensions of life that incarnate fully what it means to be human. It is walking into the self-giving of Trinitarian life this side of eternity. Running from those dimensions in life excarnates people, thereby shutting off from them a share in the divine love offered by the Godhead.

Frazier cites John McDade, "The Trinity and the Paschal Mystery," *The Heythrop Journal,* 29 (1988), pp. 175-180 as follows: "For this reason the Father loves me, because I lay down my life that I may take it again . . . this charge I have received from my Father" (Jn 10:17). The suggestion is made that the love within the divine being is a harmony of mutual self-giving which . . . is given complete expression in the events of the death and resurrection of the Son. The anticipated focus of the eternal love of Father, Son, and Spirit is that this love should be actualized within the created order, and that it should comprehend within its embrace the dimensions of creation which are threatened by death and negativity" (pp. 175-176).

"The death and resurrection of Jesus can be seen as the expression of the interchange which constitutes the divine life, and, at the same time, as the event by which the creation is brought to share in the self-giving of the Son to the Father in the mediating communion of the Holy Spirit" (p. 176).

"The thrust of recent Trinitarian theology is in the direction of viewing the events of the economy [of salvation] as effective, both for our salvation and for the dynamic of divine relatedness. According to this line of inquiry, the death and resurrection of Jesus is both the consummation of the act of the divine relationality, *and* the act by which what is created is incorporated within the intra-Trinitarian prayer and worship.

"The paschal mystery, then, is seen as both the saving incorporation of creation into the divine life and the act of mutual self-giving love among Father, Son and Spirit . . . This association of the Cross and the Trinitarian life sees in the death of Jesus the expression of a foolish wisdom which cannot be less than the self-determination of the triune God to engage the world in the mode of self-emptying love. It is in order to secure the significance of the passion and death of Jesus as an event which is expressive of the mystery of the divine being that a doctrine of the Trinity is required" (p. 177).

"The cross . . . is . . . the deepest expression of what Trinitarian life is, namely a mutual self-giving between Father and Son issuing in the inexhaustibility of the Spirit as their love" (p. 180).

3. See Bernard J. Boelen, *Personal Maturity, The Existential Dimension* (New York: The Seabury Press, 1978), pp. 6-9 and 174-82.

4. Robert Coles, *The Spirituality of Children* (Boston: Houghton Mifflin, 1990), pp. 328-29.

5. *Ibid.,* pp. 326-28.

6. Vincent Canby, "Film: Kubrick's 'Full Metal Jacket,' on Vietnam," *The New York Times*, Friday, June 26, 1987, p. C-3.

7. *The American Heritage Dictionary,* Second College Edition (Boston: Houghton Mifflin, 1985), p. 72.

4. "And as I Listen, Now I See"

1. Ouyang Xiu, "The Huamei's Song," in *A Golden Treasury of Chinese Poetry,* trans. John A. Turner, S.J., compiled and edited by John J. Deeney (Hong Kong: Renditions Paperbacks, 1989), p. 90.

2. Julia Ching, "Introduction: On Being Human and Being Chinese," *Probing China's Soul: Religion, Politics and Protest in The People's Republic* (San Francisco: Harper & Row, 1990), pp. 1-10.

3. See Thomas Merton's application of Persian psychoanalyst Reza Arasteh's understanding of cultural adaptation in William M. Thompson, *Christ and Consciousness* (New York: Paulist Press, 1979), p. 147. Elaborating on this, Thompson notes: "Cultural adaptation in Arasteh's view does not really cure illness, but only provides a way of living with it . . . A further point made by Arasteh is the distinction between anxiety which stems from the individual who has surrendered to mere cultural adaptation and thus blocked his own potential growth, and that stemming from the individual who experiences the incompleteness of such a 'cure.' The latter anxiety 'is a sign of health and generates the necessary strength for psychic rebirth into a new transcultural identity.' This identity is one in which the individual has recaptured his creativity and uniqueness, thus transcending the limitations of society and prejudice" (pp. 146-147).

Thompson quotes Merton in describing a person who has attained the "final integration" of the mature personality, not succumbing to mere cultural adaptation, but living with the anxiety that generates rebirth: "Final integration is a state of transcultural maturity far beyond mere social adjustment, which always implies partiality and compromise . . . He apprehends his life fully and wholly from an inner ground that is at once more universal than the empirical ego and yet entirely his own. He is in a certain sense 'cosmic' and 'universal man.'

"The man who has attained final integration is no longer limited by the culture in which he has grown up . . . He does not remain bound to one limited set of values in such a way that he opposes them aggressively or defensively to others. He is fully 'Catholic' in the best sense of the word... With this view of life he is able to bring perspective, liberty and spontaneity into the lives of others" (p. 147). Thompson's entire Chapter VII, "On the Need for a Trans-cultural Consciousness," pp. 128-159, offers an excellent interpretation that underscores the advantages of social misfitness vis-à-vis stretching one's consciousness beyond the confines of one's own culture or segment therein.

See also John S. Dunne, *A Search for God in Time and Memory* (Notre Dame, Indiana: University of Notre Dame Press, 1977), pp. vii-xi: "You would wonder about your basic state of mind and soul, how certain or uncertain you are, how happy or unhappy, whether you live in a state of inner assurance, a state of doubt, a state of quiet desperation. You would ask yourself ultimately about your mental image of God, what God once was to you, what he is to you now, what you expect of him.

"All these questions are quite personal and become very absorbing when you ask them. It is not easy, once you have become concerned about them, to stand back and reflect upon all this from a distance, to compare your questions and findings with those of others. The awareness that comes, nevertheless, with pursuing these very personal issues in your own life enhances greatly your ability to understand lives other than your own. You find yourself able to pass over from the standpoint of your life to those of others, entering into a sympathetic understanding of them, finding resonances between their lives and your own, and coming back once again, enriched, to your own standpoint. Many things in your life become known to you only when resonances of this kind are generated" (pp. viii-ix).

4. The way God has chosen to express the divine life through which we were created and toward which we are all called is through self-giving, self-emptying love into the Eternal Love shared among the members of the Holy Trinity. In Eternity such self-giving is in its essence self-giving and the eternal joy known of it. In time and creation this is accomplished through the openness and radical self-giving, self-emptying love demanded through suffering and death in all its forms (cf. Frazier, unpublished class notes, "The Liberating Cross").

Georges Bernanos describes the pardon God asks of us for suffering and death as the way to express the divine intention and love of the Godhead: "There is at this moment, in the world, at the back of some forsaken church, or even in an ordinary house, or at the turning of a deserted path, a poor man who joins his hands and from the depth of his misery, without very well knowing what he is saying, or without saying anything, thanks the good Lord for having made him free, for having made him capable of loving. There is somewhere else, I do not know where, a mother who hides her face for the last time in the hollow of a little breast which will beat no more, a mother next to her dead child who offers to God the groan of an exhausted resignation, as if the Voice which has thrown the suns into space as a hand throws grain, the Voice which makes the worlds tremble, had just murmured gently into her ear, "Pardon me. One day you will know, you will understand, you will give me thanks. But now, what I am looking for from you is your pardon. Pardon." These—this harassed woman, this poor man—are at the heart of the mystery, at the heart of the universal creation and in the very secret of God. What can I say of it? Language is at the service of intelligence. And what these people have understood, they have understood by a faculty superior to the intelligence although not in the least in contradiction with it—or rather, by a profound and irresistible movement of the soul which engaged all the faculties at once, which engaged to the depth their entire nature... Yes, at the moment that this man, this woman, accepted their destiny, accepted themselves, humbly—the mystery of the creation was being accomplished in them. While they were thus, without knowing it, running the entire risk of their human conduct, they were realizing themselves fully in the charity of Christ, becoming themselves, according to the words of St. Paul, other Christs. In short, they were saints." Georges Bernanos in Louis Evely, *Suffering,* trans. Marie-Claude Thompson (New York: Herder & Herder, 1967), pp. 7-8.

5. In the summer of 1989 while I was in the States not knowing if I would be allowed to return to China in the aftermath of the Tiananmen massacre and the world's response to it, I saw the film "Dead Poet's Society." The main character, a teacher of poetry in a private boarding school for boys, stood atop a desk to show how the poet views life differently, from a unique perspective. He had each of the students do this also. I was instantly frozen, remembering what I had done to illustrate the meaning of the Chinese written character for "crisis."

The film, I felt, was an encapsulation of the student democracy movement. One of the students in the film committed suicide because, among other reasons, his parents had not understood, supported, or shown any interest in his desire to become an actor. His father pressured him to change schools so he would forget this dream. The school administration scapegoated the poetry teacher as a way to cover up what was perceived as a disgrace to the school. There was no attempt to help the parents see and accept their responsibility or to deal with their grief. The denial, pretense, and deceit overflowed into the student body; their support was needed to maintain the lie. Each of the students was called into the headmaster's office, pressured to agree with the decision to scapegoat the poetry teacher by branding him as having badly influenced the boys' perception and mind-set. Expulsion was the price for not buying the headmaster's decision.

In the final scene, as the headmaster was teaching the poetry class, the poetry teacher quietly entered the classroom. He was going into his office area in the back room to get his belongings and would be leaving the school that day. The boys knew they had betrayed him. As the teacher was walking out of the classroom, one of the students stood on top of his desk and called, "O, Captain, my Captain." At first hesitantly and with fear, other students one by one did the same until all but one or two of the students in the classroom were on top of their desks, bidding farewell, acknowledging the truth and showing respect for their poetry teacher in the only and best way they could. The headmaster was shouting at them, threatening expulsion as the poetry teacher said, "Thank you, boys," and left.

The students knew the truth and felt trapped. They had to play the game of deceit abusively imposed on them by those in authority. However, those in authority could not penetrate the students' minds or hearts. They knew the truth and, with courage, let the truth be known with respect and love and hope. The film was a symbol to me of what had happened in China on June 4th and its aftermath.

6. The following from Walker Percy addresses this point: "If he [the writer] is a good poet and names something which we secretly and privately know but have not named, we rejoice at the naming and say, Yes! I know what you mean! Once again we are co-celebrants of being." Cf. Mary Deems Howland, *The Gift of the Other* (Pittsburgh: Duquesne University Press, 1990), p. 154.

7. See the following works of Alice Miller: *The Drama of the Gifted Child,* trans. Ruth Ward (New York: Basic Books, 1982); *For Your Own Good: Hidden Cruelty in Child-Rearing and the Roots of Violence*, trans. Hildegarde and Hunter Hannum (New York: Farrar Straus Giroux, 1983); and *Thou Shalt Not Be Aware: Society's Betrayal of the Child,* trans. Hildegarde and Hunter Hannum (New York: New American Library, 1984).

8. For detailed background history and accounts of the events leading up to and the aftermath of the 1989 democracy movement and the Tiananmen massacre, see Julia Ching, *Probing China's Soul*; Michael Fathers and Andrew Higgins, *Tiananmen: The Rape of Peiking* (New York: Doubleday, 1989); Han Minzhu, ed., *Cries for Democracy: Writings and Speeches from the 1989 Chinese Democracy Movement* (Princeton, N.J.: Princeton University Press, 1990); Jonathan D. Spence, *The Search for Modern China* (New York: W. W. Norton, 1990), especially Chapters 24,

"Levels of Power," and 25, "Testing the Limits," pp. 683-747; Tu Wei-Ming, "Intellectual Effervescence in China," in *Daedalus,* "The Exit from Communism," Spring 1992, pp. 251-292; and David and Peter Turnley (photographs) and Melinda Liu (text), *Beijing Spring* (Hong Kong: Asia 2000, 1989).

9. Alberto Giacometti in Matti Megged, *Dialogue in the Void—Beckett and Giacometti* (New York: Lumen Books, 1985), p. 40. In his work, Megged stresses how the vocation of the artist, whether of the word (author, Samuel Beckett) or of the hand (sculptor, Alberto Giacometti), is a struggle in the void—a struggle to bridge the gap between art and reality, to communicate the life force known to us but not within our grasp. It is a struggle doomed to failure, but the artist does not surrender. Giacometti, "in his endless efforts to find the bridge between art and reality—or even, sometimes to deny the gap between them—often insisted that he really saw the objective figure through the gaze only" (p. 40). Megged quotes Giacometti: "One does want to sculpt a living person, but what makes him alive is without a doubt his gaze...Everything else is only the framework for the gaze...If the gaze, that is, life, is the main thing...the rest of the body is limited to functioning as antennae that make people's life possible—the life that is housed in the skull..."(p. 40). Megged continues: "The head and the eye serve, in the final analysis, the impression of the gaze. But the gaze is not *seen* only by the sculptor: it is also the means of communication between the figure drawn or sculpted and the world; or, if we wish, the expression of his desire, his attempt to establish a dialogue with the invisible world, bridging the gap between them, denying the abyss. Hence the mouth of many of Giacometti's heads, open as if in a cry, or in an impossible attempt to talk with some invisible listener" (p. 42).

The 1989 Chinese democracy movement, or any movement struggling to better humanity, is, ultimately, successful to the degree that it enhances, deepens, and brings more into awareness the struggle of the artist as described in Megged's work: a struggle that takes humankind to the void—where "a fear of the void and a need for dialogue in or with the void" (p. 1) can take place.

5. "No One Ever Treated Us So Gently"

1. Marvin Bell, "These Green-Going-to-Yellow," in *The New Yorker,* November 3, 1980, p. 56.

2. *The Vatican II Weekday Missal.* Compiled by Daughters of St. Paul. (Jamaica Plain, Boston: St. Paul Editions, 1975), p. 976.

3. St. Clement, pope, from a Letter to the Corinthians, in *The Office of Readings According to the Roman Rite,* trans. International Commission on English in the Liturgy (Daughters of St. Paul, Jamaica Plain, Boston: St. Paul Editions, 1983), pp. 1196-97.

4. Flora Rheta Schreiber, *Sybil (*New York: Penguin, 1973).

5. *The Office of Readings*, p. 673.

6. Richard Giannone, *Flannery O'Connor and the Mystery of Love* (Urbana and Chicago: University of Illinois Press, 1989), p. 66.

7. *Ibid.,* p. 4.

6. "Memory Like Melody Is Pink Eternally"

1. Emily Dickinson, Poem #1578, in *The Complete Poems of Emily Dickinson,* ed. Thomas H. Johnson (Boston: Little, Brown and Company, 1960), pp. 654-655.

2. Flannery O'Connor, "A Good Man is Hard to Find," in *Flannery O'Connor: Collected Works* (New York: The Library of America, 1988), pp. 137-53.

3. Giannone, pp. 68-69.

4. *Ibid.,* p. 59

5. Miller, *The Drama of the Gifted Child,* p. 57.

6. For a detailed description of what Communism attempts and how it seems to succeed in smothering the human spirit, cf. Erazim Kohak, "Ashes, Ashes...Central Europe after Forty Years," in *Daedalus, "*The Exit from Communism," Spring 1992, pp. 197-215.

7. O'Connor, "A Good Man Is Hard to Find," p. 152.

8. Giannone, p. 50.

9. *Ibid.,* pp. 50-51.

10. *Ibid.,* p. 47.

11. *Ibid.,* p. 52.

12. *Ibid.,* pp. 52-53.

13. *Ibid.,* pp. 52-53.

SUGGESTED READINGS

Including Sources Quoted and Consulted

Bell, Marvin. "These Green-Going-to-Yellow." *The New Yorker,* November 3, 1980, p. 56.

Boelen, Bernard J. *Personal Maturity, The Existential Dimension.* New York: The Seabury Press, 1978.

Breslin, John B., S.J. "Vision and Revision: Seamus Heaney's New Poems." *America,* December 7, 1991, p. 438.

Canby, Vincent. "Film: Kubrick's 'Full Metal Jacket,' on Vietnam." *The New York Times,* Friday, June 26, 1987, p. C-3.

Ching, Julia. *Probing China's Soul: Religion, Politics and Protest in The People's Republic.* San Francisco: Harper & Row, 1990.

Coles, Robert. *The Spirituality of Children.* Boston: Houghton Mifflin, 1990.

Dunne, John S. *A Search for God in Time and Memory.* Notre Dame, Indiana: University of Notre Dame Press, 1977.

Evely, Louis. *Suffering.* Trans. Marie-Claude Thompson. New York: Herder & Herder, 1967.

Fathers, Michael and Andrew Higgins. *Tiananmen: The Rape of Peiking.* New York: Doubleday, 1989.

Faulkner, William. *Essays, Speeches and Public Letters.* Ed. James A. Meriwether. New York: Random House, 1965.

Frazier, William B., M.M. "Priesthood and Brotherhood in Maryknoll: Missiological Foundations." Unpublished manuscript. Maryknoll, NY, 1994.

————— "The Liberating Cross," lecture notes from a course offered at Maryknoll School of Theology, Maryknoll, NY, Autumn 1994.

Fung Yu-lan. *A Short History of Chinese Philosophy.* Ed. Derk Bodde. New York: The Free Press, 1966.

Gardner, John. *The Art of Living and Other Stories.* New York: Knopf, 1981.

Giannone, Richard. *Flannery O'Connor and the Mystery of Love.* Urbana and Chicago: University of Illinois Press, 1989.

Hammarskjold, Dag. *Markings*. Trans. Leif Sjoberg and W. H. Auden. New York: Knopf, 1976.

Han Minzhu, ed. *Cries for Democracy: Writings and Speeches from the 1989 Chinese Democracy Movement*. Princeton, NJ: Princeton University Press, 1990.

Howland, Mary Deems. *The Gift of the Other*. Pittsburgh: Duquesne University Press, 1990.

Johnson, Thomas H., ed. *The Complete Poems of Emily Dickinson*. Boston: Little, Brown and Company, 1960.

Koch, Kenneth. *I Never Told Anybody: Teaching Poetry Writing in a Nursing Home*. New York: Random House, 1977.

Kohak, Erazim. "Ashes, Ashes...Central Europe after Forty Years." *Daedalus*, "The Exit from Communism," Spring 1992.

Lindbergh, Anne Morrow. *Hour of Gold, Hour of Lead*. New York: Harcourt Brace Jovanovich, 1973.

McDade, John. "The Trinity and the Paschal Mystery." *The Heythrop Journal*, 29 (1988).

Megged, Matti. *Dialogue in the Void—Beckett and Giacometti*. New York: Lumen Books, 1985.

Merton, Thomas. *Mystics and Zen Masters*. New York: Delta, 1967.

Midler, Bette. "Fried Eggs," from *Bette Midler Live at Last*. Atlantic Recording Corporation, NY, 1977; Divine's Music Ltd., BMI.

Miller, Alice. *The Drama of the Gifted Child*. Trans. Ruth Ward. New York: Basic Books, 1982.

———. *For Your Own Good: Hidden Cruelty in Child-Rearing and the Roots of Violence*. Trans. Hildegarde and Hunter Hannum. New York: Farrar Straus Giroux, 1983.

———. *Thou Shalt Not Be Aware: Society's Betrayal of the Child*. Trans. Hildegarde and Hunter Hannum. New York: New American Library, 1984.

O'Connor, Flannery. "A Good Man is Hard to Find." *Flannery O'Connor: Collected Works*. New York: The Library of America, 1988.

———. *Mystery and Manners; Occasional Prose*. Selected and edited by Sally and Robert Fitzgerald. New York: Farrar, Straus & Giroux, 1979.

The Office of Readings According to the Roman Rite. Daughters of St. Paul, Jamaica Plain, Boston: St. Paul Editions, 1983.

Ouyang Xiu, "The Huamei's Song." *A Golden Treasury of Chinese Poetry*. Trans. John A. Turner, S.J. Compiled and edited by John J. Deeney. Hong Kong: Renditions, 1989.

Schreiber, Flora Rheta. *Sybil*. New York: Penguin, 1973.

Spence, Jonathan D. *The Search for Modern China*. New York: W. W. Norton, 1990.

Thompson, William M. *Christ and Consciousness.* New York: Paulist Press, 1979.

Tracy, David. *The Analogical Imagination.* New York: Crossroad, 1981.

Tu Wei-Ming. "Intellectual Effervescence in China." *Daedalus,* "The Exit from Communism," Spring 1992.

Turnley, David and Peter (photographs) and Melinda Liu (text). *Beijing Spring.* Hong Kong: Asia 2000, 1989.

The Vatican II Weekday Missal. Compiled by Daughters of St. Paul. Jamaica Plain, Boston: St. Paul Editions, 1975.

Walsh, Bishop James Edward, M.M. "Description of a Missioner." Maryknoll, NY: Development Department, 1976.

Williams, Oscar, ed. *Immortal Poems of the English Language.* New York: Washington Square Press, 1952.